T0355844

52 WAYS TO RECONCILE

HOW TO WALK WITH INDIGENOUS PEOPLES ON THE PATH TO HEALING

DAVID A. ROBERTSON

McClelland & Stewart

McClelland & Stewart and colophon are registered trademarks of Penguin Random House Canada Limited.

The authorized representative in the EU for product safety and compliance is Penguin Random House Ireland, Morrison Chambers, 32 Nassau Street, Dublin D02 YH68, Ireland, https://eu-contact.penguin.ie

Library and Archives Canada Cataloguing in Publication data is available upon request.

ISBN: 978-0-7710-1935-7
ebook ISBN: 978-0-7710-1943-2

Selected pieces originally appeared in *Cottage Life*: "Research Indigenous Place Names" (May 2023); "Attend a Powwow" (May 2022); "The Difference between cultural appreciation and appropriation" (June/July 2021).

Cover design by Matthew Flute
Interior art: Graficriver – stock.adobe.com
Typeset in Baskerville by Terra Page
Printed in the United States of America

McClelland & Stewart
A division of Penguin Random House Canada
320 Front Street West, Suite 1400
Toronto, Ontario, M5V 3B6, Canada
penguinrandomhouse.ca

1 2 3 4 5   29 28 27 26 25

Penguin
Random House
McCLELLAND & STEWART

I am only one, but still I am one. I cannot do everything, but still I can do something and because I cannot do everything, I will not refuse to do the something that I can do.

—EDWARD EVERETT HALE

CONTENTS

52 WAYS TO RECONCILE

INTRODUCTION

MY FIRST PUBLISHED book, *Stone*, came out in March 2010—book one in a graphic novel series entitled 7 Generations. Before that, I had self-published, in partnership with the Helen Betty Osborne Memorial Foundation, a graphic novel entitled *The Life of Helen Betty Osborne*. That was in 2008. The first several books I published through HighWater Press in Winnipeg were short graphic novels. I intentionally decided to focus on comics because they have done a lot of damage through their representation of Indigenous people and history over the last seventy years or so. I have always had the mindset that we should fight fire with fire. Following that logic, if comics had done damage, why could they not also undo that damage? If comics stereotyped Indigenous people and trivialized our many distinct cultures and languages, and our place in history, they could also do the opposite. Since 2010, graphic novels and comic books have become a go-to medium for many Indigenous writers and illustrators across Turtle Island, one of many forms of literature, and within those forms, genres that Indigenous creators have embraced to tell our stories. The overarching goal, as I see it, is at once damage control and sharing knowledge so that people, children and adults, are better prepared to do the work of reconciliation.

However, it is sometimes hard to understand the work of reconciliation because the term itself can be difficult to define. So, if we are going to discuss reconciliation and what our roles are and can be, we ought to define it as best we can. It's a relatively new term insofar as it's applied to Canada and its relationship with Indigenous Peoples, coming into prominence in 2008 with the creation of the Truth and Reconciliation Commission (TRC). Since 2008, it has become ubiquitous and inextricably tied to the long-term goal of healing the relationship between Indigenous Peoples and Canada at large. However, in being used so widely and indiscriminately, it has started to lose its lustre and meaning. As a result, we are in danger of losing our focus, and maybe even, in the not-so-distant future, our interest. That is something we cannot afford. After all, when you look at things objectively, we have come so far in a relatively short period. Just think about how, in a decade, we have gone from barely talking about the Indian Residential School System in schools to teaching it at almost every grade level, from coast to coast to coast. You cannot visit a school in Canada and find students who do not know about the Indian Residential School System. Trust me. I speak to tens of thousands of kids every year. I suppose what scares me is that all of this will become rote, because if it does, it will mean less, and if it means less, if we act with less intention, we will not get to where we need to be. For reconciliation to work, we need everybody, and we need everybody to be passionate about it.

Let's start with the word *reconciliation*. It is likely that I will mention my father, Donald Robertson, several times in this book, so it makes sense to get that out of the way early. Dad and I used to discuss reconciliation often. We talked about what it was, what it ought to be, and what it involved for everybody, acknowledging that we all have different roles, whether you are an Indigenous person or a non-Indigenous person. Technically, reconciliation is defined as the restoration of friendly relations. Two good friends become estranged for whatever reason, and after many years, find their way back to each other, and one sees the other as a friend once more. There was a good relationship, something caused it to fracture, and then a healing occurred and the relationship was restored. The two people reconciled. Now, this is not intended to be a history book, but there is enough evidence and academic work to support the claim that between Indigenous Peoples and colonists, there never was a right relationship. If there was not a good relationship to begin with, what exactly are we restoring? The work that we are trying to do, then, is to develop a strong and healthy relationship for the first time. Don't get me wrong: I believe that we are getting there, but reconciliation is something of a misnomer. At the time of my father's passing in December 2019, he and a group of Elders, or grandparents, as he liked to refer to them, were trying to come up with a term that better suited the act. Maybe one of the acts to reconcile is spending time thinking about what a suitable term might be, but that doesn't seem as active as I want it to be, so for the sake of argument, keeping in mind that we are working with an imperfect term, let's go with it. Let's focus on how to build something together that is lasting because it will be on a solid foundation. The last thing Dad said to me was to ask, "Aren't there more important things to worry about right now?" His point is well taken. If we worry too much about a term, we may lose sight of the action that is required.

That is one thing I know for sure. *Reconciliation* is an action. I know that as much as I know that each of us has a role to play; it's just that we have different roles. Part of how we move forward is to understand truth, accept it, and then fully explore what our role is. That's emblematic of a community; we don't all do the same thing, and if we did, some things would not get done. There is no job that is smaller or bigger than another. I'm a hockey dad, so pardon the analogy, but there are positions to play. You have yours, and I have mine, and when everybody figures out what position they have, and how to play that position most effectively, we have a better chance of winning. And you have to believe, as a community, if we do this right, we all win.

So, what are our roles?

"You cannot heal brokenness from a place of brokenness."

That's what a principal at Jack River School in Norway House Cree Nation told me a few years ago when I was visiting the community and speaking to students at the school. She was talking about teachers working hard to enrich the lives of children in the community but dealing with their own trauma, and how difficult it was to help children navigate trauma from a place of personal, unresolved pain. I've thought a lot about that since our conversation, and what I have come to understand and see in my own life as well is that Indigenous people have healing to do from the impacts of colonialism. I do not speak my father's first language, Swampy Cree, due to the impacts of colonialism, both in his life and the life of my grandmother. My road to healing has been to be an active participant in the movement towards language revitalization—every book of mine since 2018 has

Swampy Cree in it. I want kids to feel motivated to learn their language, and I am learning a little bit myself, too. We all have more work to do, living through the very loud echo of intergenerational trauma, and it's hard. We need time and space to do that work.

There is the larger movement we have known as reconciliation, which is the development of a good relationship between Indigenous and non-Indigenous people, but for Indigenous people, there is also reconciliation needed within communities, families, and the individual. I would argue that one must take precedence over the other. That is not to say we do not have a larger role to play in reconciliation. We are meant to be storytellers, to share truths so that other people have the knowledge required to take meaningful action. Jody Wilson-Raybould articulates this process very well in her book *True Reconciliation*.

If the role of Indigenous people is to be storytellers, what is your role? Because there is no question that you have one. Reconciliation is a community effort, and for it to work, it's all hands on deck. As individuals, we have considerable influence. If we are complacent and do nothing, other people will do nothing. If we are active and do something, we will inspire other people to do something. And there is so much to do. This movement is far-reaching. The IRSS will always be at the heart of it, but it also involves the colonial history and contemporary barriers of this country, from foster care and the Sixties Scoop to health care to justice and epidemics like Missing and Murdered Indigenous Women, Girls, and Two-Spirit People (MMIWG2S). It is a Canadian issue, and if you are Canadian, you have a responsibility to get involved. This is not to say that you should feel guilt or shame, but it is to say that you can and should act.

How do you know what action to take? How do you know what is meaningful action and what is not? If there is one thing I've learned, it's that Canadians want to do the right thing. The barrier is that there can be a fear of doing the *wrong* thing. It's a conundrum. That's how we learn, though. Don't forget that this is all still new, and because it's new, we are going to make mistakes along the way. All of us, as a community. The farther we get, the more we learn, the better we will do.

If we're doing this together, we must shoulder the weight together. We can't do that if we aren't willing to support one another. And so, I've put this book together for you. Let's call it an activity book. There's something here that you can do every week for an entire year that will contribute to fixing the mess that has been made. These actions are (mostly) not in any specific order. You can do any of them at any time, at your leisure, remembering that some of them are tied to particular days (for example, the National Day for Truth and Reconciliation). Some of them are harder than others. Some of them are kind of fun. Who doesn't like reading a good book? And going to a powwow is a beautiful experience. All of them are meaningful.

I'll leave you to it. Just remember that we're walking together every step of the way. That's how it needs to be done.

Week #1

HOST A MOVIE NIGHT

WHAT I WANT for the publishing industry—for Indigenous people to be equitably represented in all areas, from graphic design to marketing to editorial, not just authors and illustrators—is what I want in every industry, from education to the arts. What will help lead to parity (that is, if Indigenous people make up 12 percent of the Canadian population, 12 percent of all books published should be by an Indigenous writer) is increased demand. Put simply, the more you buy books by Indigenous authors, the more publishers will want to publish them. Following that logic, the more you watch Indigenous television shows, the more you watch Indigenous movies, the more shows and films will get made with the involvement of Indigenous people. And not just actors, not just directors, not just writers. What you've seen with recent productions that tell Indigenous stories is that Indigenous people are getting hired for all positions. *Reservation Dogs*, for example, had an all-Indigenous writers' room, an all-Indigenous main cast, and an all-Indigenous crew. I could be really short here and just say, "Watch a movie that has, as close as possible, that same level of representation," but I'm going to give you a few suggestions along the way.

There's an addition to the house my family lives in—a sunroom—that juts out into our backyard. A couple of years ago, I bought a manual pull-down screen so that we can project movies onto it while we sit around the firepit when the sun goes down and it's dark enough to see the images on the white vinyl. Often, we'll invite neighbours over, and we'll have hot dogs and maybe even s'mores and *definitely* chips. If we have a movie night in the winter, we grab a bunch of blankets, make finger food, and cuddle up in the family room (I'll 100 percent fall asleep, but if you've seen my wife's social media posts, you know that me falling asleep pretty much anywhere is also family tradition).

So, here's where we're at: You either already have a movie night, which is convenient, or you don't, and all that means is you have to plan to have at least one movie night (but hopefully a couple, because I'm about to give you three or four suggestions, and you don't only have to watch just one).

The first film that comes to mind is the first film I can remember watching that had authentic Indigenous characters in it from an authentic Indigenous perspective (it's filmed on location on the Coeur d'Alene Reservation in Idaho), which is why it walks the very delicate line between drama and comedy quite expertly. We do that very well. Coincidentally, it is also the first feature-length film written by, directed by, produced by, and starring Indigenous people to reach a wide audience domestically and internationally. I'm talking about *Smoke Signals*, which stars a familiar cast of characters in Adam Beach, Evan Adams, Gary Farmer, Irene Bedard, and Tantoo

Cardinal; the movie also marked the debut of Chris Eyre, who has gone on to produce and/or direct thirteen films. The story is about two young men, Victor and Thomas, who have differing views of Victor's father, Arnold. Arnold is a hero, but also an alcoholic and an abuser. When he dies, the two friends set off on a road trip to retrieve Arnold's ashes, eventually spreading them into a river as a form of healing and acceptance. It really is a beautiful film that deserves to be seen.

Smoke Signals came out in 1998. Three years later, one of the best Indigenous films that has been made was released: *Atanarjuat: The Fast Runner*. Like the previous film, *Atanarjuat* is not only great but also culturally significant. It was the first feature film to be written, directed, produced, and acted entirely in the Inuktitut language. The crew was reportedly 90 percent Inuit. *Atanarjuat* premiered at Cannes, where it won the Caméra d'Or, and then went on to win six Genie Awards, which is Canada's equivalent of the Academy Awards. In 2015 it was named, in canvassing filmmakers and critics, the greatest Canadian film of all time. Not too bad. It's always good to be, as the kids say, the GOAT. *Atanarjuat* is a retelling of an Inuit legend at least one thousand years old that, like oral stories across Indigenous cultures, has been passed down from generation to generation. The screenplay was based on versions of the same Inuit legend told by eight Elders. I'd call the plot somewhat Shakespearean, but it predates Shakespeare. It's a long film, and the way it's shot makes it feel more like a documentary, but the best stories, in my opinion, provide a glimpse into the lives of others. What better way to do this than to present a film as though you're watching a real-life experience? In watching the film, you will learn about culture and stories and have a literal window into the lives of people you would not have otherwise learned about.

Like Captain America, I could do this all day; there are many films to choose from, and there are more and more each year, which is something I never thought I'd see. But here we are. I'm going to focus on, appropriately, the newest film I've watched, seeing as how I started out with the first film I viewed with Indigenous people in control.

There's been this cool thing that's happened in the arts over the last few years. It's not just that we have increasing control over the stories we tell as Indigenous people; it's that we are telling stories that cross over into genres you wouldn't typically expect to find Indigenous stories in. *Blood Quantum* is a Canadian horror film that was written, directed, and edited by the late Jeff Barnaby, who died of cancer in 2022. Barnaby was Mi'kmaq. The film, like others on this list, is filled with Indigenous talent in all aspects of development, including an excellent cast that boasts the red-hot Devery Jacobs, who has recently been seen in *Reservation Dogs* and the Marvel Cinematic Universe television series *Echo*. In *Blood Quantum*, Indigenous people cannot be infected by a zombie uprising. In the same brilliant way that several Indigenous stories have been able to make social commentary while flipping things around in thought-provoking ways, in this film white refugees begin to seek safety on a reserve. It's kind of satisfying to watch a movie where non-Indigenous characters are envious of the Indigenous population, but it's also a clever commentary on issues that are going on in Canada today, like the ongoing struggle with "pretendians." It's a dark film, and disturbing, but as an Indigenous person it's hard not to feel excited and swell with pride to see a movie like this, knowing that it will create more films, in other genres, that will be created, executed, and delivered with Indigenous people at the helm.

Throw on the popcorn, make yourself comfortable, and pick an Indigenous movie that will undoubtedly entertain as much as, if you look below the surface, it educates. Just make sure that real, live Indigenous people were in control of the creative process—from writing to directing to crew to actors—because that's how you're going to find the best stories told from a place of authenticity.

Week #2

START AN INDIGENOUS BOOK CLUB

IF THE FOUNDATION of reconciliation is stories, which I think it is, we need to have a few more specific actions related to this healing process that directly involve storytelling. There's a barrier to this, and it's a good one. It's one we wouldn't have encountered as recently as fifteen years ago—give or take. How are we ever going to choose a book for an Indigenous book club? There are so many books out there right now about Indigenous people, by Indigenous people. And those are the criteria for this book club. In fact, these are the only criteria we should be concerned with. Whatever book you choose, it needs to be about Indigenous people, and it needs to be written by an Indigenous author.

I know. That leaves a lot of options, but don't overthink it. Let me overthink it for you, at least to start. I'm an expert at overthinking; I have anxiety, after all. In all seriousness, there are a lot of things to sift through before choosing the right book to start a club with. A good question is, "What kind of book do I want to read?" Because just saying you want to read an Indigenous book doesn't give you a lot to go on. In Canada today, even though we still don't have quite the equitable share in the publishing world that we should have, we're getting there, and that means there are many books being published by Indigenous writers, about several different subjects, and in a number of different genres.

I searched "Indigenous writers in Canada" on the internet and got forty-two authors in less than a second. It was a good mix, too. Poets, novelists, children's authors, young and old, Métis, and a number of First Nations are represented. There's the late great Richard Wagamese, and another icon I idolized growing up, Thomas King. In that group of trailblazers were also Tomson Highway, Michelle Good, Maria Campbell, Harold R. Johnson, Lee Maracle, and Beatrice Mosionier. Then there are the likes of Cherie Dimaline, katherena vermette, Billy-Ray Belcourt, Joshua Whitehead, Richard Van Camp, Waubgeshig Rice and Wab Kinew (just to get the Wabs out of the way), Tanya Tagaq and Tanya Talaga (likewise for the Tanyas), Warren Cariou (my first Indigenous editor), Eden Robinson, Niigaanwewidam Sinclair, and so many more (I'm going to stop because I know I'll forget somebody and it'll bother me for days). There are children's authors, too. Monique Gray Smith, Julie Flett, Melanie Florence, Jenny Kay Dupuis, Nicola I. Campbell, and Phyllis Webstad. There's even a guy named David A. Robertson, although under his name, there's a picture of some smiley white dude in a shirt and tie and a Casio watch (I love that watch, though).

See what I mean? There are a lot of us, and more are getting published all the time. But what will help narrow things down isn't asking who we should read but rather what we should read about. From there, we can whittle it down a bit more until we come up with a first choice. I've written a lot already about how reconciliation is a movement that has countless moving parts; it is not only about the Indian Residential School System, although that will always, and should always, be the centrepiece. It's about community building, which stories do. It's about representation, which stories are also especially good at. It's about addressing the historical and contemporary trauma of Indigenous people in colonial Canada, beyond the Indian Residential School System. There are stories that offer those teachings, but there is also learning about Indigenous people, families, experiences, and communities without looking through the lens of trauma. It might be there, of course, but it's not what drives the story forward. It's not the reason why the story is being told. It's equally important to learn about all the beautiful things that Indigenous people are and what we can offer. Cultures, languages, ways of living, values, beliefs, traditions, and, weaving all of this together, Story.

Let's talk about Richard Wagamese. The first book in your new Indigenous Book Club, the last book that Richard wrote, and one that remains unfinished, is *Starlight*.

Why *Starlight*?

It is a novel that, while heavy with trauma—it addresses spousal abuse and the foster care system—is not anchored by that trauma. Rather, it's anchored by characters with agency or who develop agency, and the relationships that build between humans who happen to be Indigenous and non-Indigenous. Finally, it's a story that displays all the characteristics of a strong, stereotype-breaking Indigenous character, in such a way that articulates, better than any novel I've ever read, the concept of Blood Memory. Blood

Memory is when the lives and experiences of your ancestors live within you, woven into the fabric of your DNA.

Frank Starlight is a protagonist who continually (in a non-repetitive way) refuses to acknowledge his Indigeneity as a source for his connection to the land, but who clearly feels that connection because of who he is: a strong, generous, capable, gentle Indigenous man. Starlight presents the reader with an alternative to the stereotypical image of the Indigenous character we are so familiar with in popular culture.

Frank is richly Indigenous but is not bound by any one concept of what being Indigenous is, or what it should be. There is so much to unpack in this novel, not the least of which is a discussion of where the story was headed when it abruptly but poignantly ends. It leaves the reader with characters that are so well written that they live on; in turn, it is left to the reader to decide what will happen in the story, and it presents, as gifts, characters that can live on with us.

Please know that whatever book you choose, it will offer you something important. As long as it is a book about Indigenous people, by an Indigenous author, to ensure accuracy, truth, and autonomy in the characters and their journey.

Week #3

ENGAGE WITH INDIGENOUS SOCIAL MEDIA

SOCIAL MEDIA CAN be a toxic environment. It wasn't always that way, but you have to be cognizant of it now. A common problem is that immediate information has led to immediate reaction. Reaction without all the information. There are far too many examples, but suffice it to say that when I see something trending on social media, I've trained myself to wait a day or two before reacting, if I do at all, because there will always be more information that recontextualizes an incident or event. In the Indigenous community, it might be that somebody is called out for being a "pretendian" (a non-Indigenous person passing themselves off as an Indigenous person). There is an immediate reaction, and while the revelation can often be true, there have been times when it is not. It harms the community, and it possibly damages a person's reputation unnecessarily. Following accounts of people who share measured responses based on facts can help to navigate a divisive, difficult, and growing issue.

But social media can also be an incredible source of information. Some accounts avoid toxicity altogether, and instead focus on positive and empowering topics. There are accounts that share Indigenous languages—words of the day—and this helps both in language revitalization and in teaching non-Indigenous people some words in a language. Some accounts share upcoming events that you can mark on your calendar, like Indigenous concerts, Indigenous book festivals, and Indigenous conferences or gatherings, and if you can't make it due to geography or time constraints, there are often accounts that have summarized or live-tweeted presentations, or filmed and shared moments (when it's appropriate to do so). Some accounts will address a complex issue and break it down so that it's easy to understand if you don't have background or experience.

Social media can be an effective way to mobilize. Following the right people online can help you find out about gatherings, marches, or protests that are happening in your area, that you can attend and take part in. While social media can be used to quickly spread disinformation, it's also one of the most effective ways to quickly and efficiently pull people together when something has happened that necessitates that kind of response. I'm thinking here about a recent incident in response to a call to ban books about sexual orientation and gender identity from all classrooms and libraries, led by a former school trustee and grandmother, and directed toward the Brandon School Division. Hundreds of people came together to ensure that this ban was voted down by trustees, and it was, in a 6–1 vote. Many people, I am certain, found out about the meeting online and chose to attend as a result. Without the presence of a community of concerned people, who knows how that vote might have gone. Mobilizing doesn't have to be done physically, either. People can come together online, and social media is a good way to accomplish this. When *The Great Bear* was banned, a board meeting was held in person and online. People were able to ask questions online (although the organizers controlled what questions were read aloud) that were answered by those responsible for pulling the book. I, along with other interested parties, shared news of the public meeting, and though I don't know the number of people that "showed up," I do know it would have been a healthy audience that came out to support the return of *The Great Bear* to classrooms and libraries.

I've loved making contact with teachers, students, and readers on social media and sharing aspects of my family life that help people feel more connected to me. Again, I'm a big believer in community, and making those connections is vital in the process of community building. I love going to education conferences and having teachers come up to me, just wanting to say hi because they feel like they know me (and they do). Some of the educators and readers who follow me have also found their way to my wife, who is much funnier and more engaging on social media. Many people are aware that I tend to fall asleep at weird times and in weird places because my wife posts videos of me after I've nodded off, snoring on a chair at the dining room table, or sitting outside by the pool with a book on my chest. Social media is a place to learn about upcoming releases, albums, books, movies, or shows. And artists may share some of their work. I've done online readings on various social media platforms, given writing tips, and participated in interviews with other authors. I'm a fan, too. I follow a lot of accounts for Indigenous artists so I can benefit just like you can. There's a traditional dancer

I follow on TikTok named James Jones, and I love the quick and clever performances they do.

The pandemic gave us some good things, despite all the awful experiences that many people endured. The way that people interact online has changed. Sure, some of it can be problematic. But if you sift through that negativity, you can find cool people that you can learn a lot from, and that you can engage with. If reconciliation is an action, and that action involves us getting to know one another, it's important that we find ways to do that. We can't always sit across from one another and share stories, so connecting online is an opportunity that we should take advantage of. Stories are stories. However we find them, they illuminate a path we're all following together, side by side, to achieve the long-term goal of healing through healthy relationships built on a foundation of truth, knowledge, empathy, and respect.

Week #4

LEARN THE DIFFERENCE BETWEEN CULTURAL APPROPRIATION AND CULTURAL APPRECIATION

SOME OF MY BEST and earliest memories are of the lake. Starting when I was a baby, I went with my family to Riding Mountain National Park in Manitoba every summer and stayed at a little resort with housekeeping cottages. When my wife and I had kids of our own, we continued the tradition, bringing our kids to the lake in August and staying at the same place. The cabins encircle a communal area where there are picnic benches, firepits, and a lamp post that I broke one year with an errant Frisbee. There's a play structure for kids with a few slides and a sandbox. The swimming pool is always warm—it's never the wrong time for a swim, whatever the weather.

At the front of it all, a totem pole stands facing the road. At the end of the week, all the Robertsons would line up in front of it for a family picture. As I got older, I began to question some of the things I grew up with at the lake. It troubled me, more and more, that Indigenous cultures were treated as though they were nothing more than tourist attractions—curiosities at best, empty and meaningless at worst. Worse than that, it's completely out of place. Totem poles originate from Indigenous Peoples of the Pacific Northwest. There's already a relatively common view that Indigenous cultures are a monolith, and inaccuracies like this do nothing to dispel that falsehood. As I worked to educate myself on issues that Indigenous people face, that nagging feeling became clear, and the question I kept asking was, "Is this cultural appropriation?"

That question is a good starting point. We should make a habit of asking it more often, especially once we've been made aware that a name, a monument, a piece of jewellery, an item of clothing, or even a watercraft, such as a kayak, might be problematic. Inquisitiveness indicates a desire to learn. A simple willingness to know and bravery to ask questions when uncertain can help shift an act of appropriation into one of appreciation.

The distinction between cultural appropriation and cultural appreciation is relatively straightforward: it's an act of appropriation when someone uses an aspect of a culture that's not their own without understanding or respecting it, especially when it's a historically oppressed group and when it involves personal gain or profit. Appreciation, on the other hand, sees people genuinely trying to learn about and understand another culture in order to broaden their perspective. It builds relationships across different cultures and involves asking permission and giving credit and fair compensation.

Profit doesn't necessarily mean monetary gain. The other day, I was scrolling through TikTok, and I came across a video of a dancing model wearing a bikini, a headdress, and war paint. Ostensibly, this individual was trying to get "likes." If you're borrowing from an Indigenous culture for profit or attention, it's an act of appropriation, and it doesn't have to be deliberate or malicious. In most cases, nobody's trying to do harm. Putting an inukshuk on the front steps of your cottage. Buying dreamcatcher earrings from the shop in town because they look nice on you.

"What's the big deal?"

That's a question I often get in my line of work, and the stakes are higher than it might seem. Addressing appropriation is necessary if we genuinely wish to work towards healing as a community. It's an integral part of the process of reconciliation. Healing requires us to listen to, learn from, and understand each other. When you know better, you do better.

If you've placed an inukshuk on your property, do some research. When you have a guest over, and they notice the beautiful structure on your doorstep, you can thank them and explain that inuksuit are used in the north by Inuit for a number of reasons, including as a navigation tool to guide people across the tundra, a signpost to mark a cache or a good hunting or fishing spot, and a message board to communicate something such as a change from an intended route. When you buy those dreamcatcher earrings, take the time to ask the person who made them about their meaning. Learn enough about them so that you can articulate their meaning to somebody else. And oh. That person who made them? Make sure they're Indigenous and that the dreamcatcher is *authentic*.

What about totem poles? They're typically made out of red cedar and represent ancestry, history, people, or events. They display beings or crest animals that mark a family's lineage. They are visual representations of kinship. Just, you know, not in Manitoba.

My best and earliest memories are of the lake. So were Dad's. He loved the calm of being near the water; it reminded him of his childhood on the trapline. Maybe your memories are of the lake, too. My dad used to say that we're all human beings, and we share far more than we think. Let's move forward together with that in mind and ensure, as much as we can, that the time we spend and the memories we cherish don't come at the expense of somebody else's culture.

Week #5

RESEARCH INDIGENOUS PLACE NAMES

THERE'S A RIVER just across the street from my house. When I go outside in the morning, it smells and feels like I'm at the cottage. I love that. In the summer, my wife kayaks on it, sometimes with our youngest kid on her lap. In the winter, a neighbour sets up a hockey rink, and kids from the block play shinny. I can hear their laughter and the ice churn from their skate blades from my doorstep.

The waterway is called the Assiniboine, one of two major rivers that wind through Winnipeg. This name is of Indigenous origin, as many placenames are in this country. That doesn't cross the minds of many Canadians, but it should. One of the joys of being in nature is the connection to place. A recognition that we are as much a part of it as the fish, birds, and four-legged creatures.

The Assiniboine River's name comes from the Assiniboine people, whose traditional lands are southwestern Manitoba, southeastern Saskatchewan, and northern Montana and North Dakota. The word means "those who cook by placing hot stones in water." It took only a few minutes to research that. In doing so, I have become even more in tune with where I am. Discovering the meaning of the word has, in turn, strengthened what the river and where I live means to me.

There's a benefit to figuring out whether or not the name of your lake is in an Indigenous language or derives from an Indigenous word. Lake Winnipeg and Lake Ontario fall under that category. Those two names don't sound Indigenous, but they are. *Winnipeg* is a word that comes from a Cree phrase that translates to "muddy waters." *Ontario* comes from a Haudenosaunee word, *kanadario*, which means "sparkling water." One of the things I love about Indigenous names for places, for waterways, is that they are beautiful but also literal. If you look out over Lake Ontario on a sunny day, the water glimmers like a field of diamonds.

I have an ulterior motive for suggesting that you explore the history of the place names in your area. I've found, in the course of my career, that fostering connections creates accountability. Our lands and waters are sick, and even if we don't agree on everything, we must agree that we need to do whatever we can to keep them healthy. So, what are some lakes and rivers around you that you could learn more about and connect to?

Do some research; online is a good place to start. I used the Canadian Encyclopedia, the Great Lakes Guide, and Britannica. I compiled information and then compared it so I knew it was accurate. I'd also suggest connecting to local communities with knowledge keepers and speakers who can translate and maybe even add a bit more depth to those translations. In my experience, Indigenous people are welcoming of this sort of effort to understand. I am.

Is the lake or river's name a First Nations name? If so, what does it mean? If not, can you find out what the name was before it was renamed? Connecting to your waterways will generate the intention to protect them, just as it did for the Indigenous people who have cared for them for thousands of years.

WRITE A LAND ACKNOWLEDGEMENT

LAND ACKNOWLEDGEMENTS ARE no longer uncommon. They used to be. When I first started doing public presentations, visiting schools, and working with teachers, I never heard them. We've come a long way in a short period of time. I live in Winnipeg, and prior to a hockey or football game, a conference, an assembly, or any number of events, a land acknowledgement is recited. I think it's great that we do this, and I know that Winnipeg isn't the only place this is done, but I intentionally used the word *recited*. Recitation is the act of repeating something from memory or from a phrase that has been written down and used before. And I wonder: If we recite something, does it mean as much, or enough? I don't think it does. We have to be careful that in our progress, we don't regress by making important actions rote. It's like driving home from work. You take the route so many times that some days, you don't even remember getting home, and yet there you are, in front of your house.

To recite something is to lack intention, and that's what I think we're beginning to miss. If we don't have intention, the action becomes less meaningful—maybe even, at some point down the line, meaningless. It will become a chore. Nobody likes chores.

Lately, I've been a proponent of writing land acknowledgements from scratch, because it forces us to really look at things, to learn and understand things, that will inevitably lead to a personal connection and investment. I've worked with businesses, administrators, teachers, librarians, and students to go over some of the main boxes we need to check in order to write a good land acknowledgement. The end goal is to commit to some sort of reciprocity. The land has given to us, so what can we give to it in return, to ensure its long-term health? That should be a significant concern for everybody; if the land isn't healthy, if we continue to abuse its resources, we're in big trouble.

So, what does a proper land acknowledgement look like? The kind I often hear now goes something like this: *We acknowledge that we are gathered on ancestral lands, Treaty 1 territory, the traditional territory of the Anishinaabeg, Cree, Oji-Cree, Dakota, and Dene Peoples, and on the National Homeland of the Red River Métis.* Okay. That's fine. My question is: What does it accomplish, and how can we go further?

The acknowledgement I cut and pasted—which I find is usually what's done: we cut and paste and recite—is a good starting point. We need to know where our feet are planted. Are you on treaty land or on unceded territory, and what do either of those two things mean? What is a treaty, and if you are on treaty land, what treaty? It's easy to find out; there are resources that list the numerous treaties across Turtle Island, what we now call Canada. And it'll take a bit of time, but it's easy to read through the applicable treaty, too. A lot was given by Indigenous Peoples, and not much was provided in return. Education for kids, the reserve system, and maybe five dollars annually without inflation (I just caught up on thirteen years of unclaimed treaty payments and got a whopping sixty-five dollars in my bank account).

It boils down to relationships. We build healthy relationships with one another if you take the time to learn about me, and I take the time to learn about you. In that spirit, a land acknowledgement should look at the historical caretakers of the land you're on, but more than that, should acknowledge who is still here today. Once that's done, think of ways that you can make meaningful connections, to create partnerships built on mutual respect and understanding. A friend of my father, Strini Reddy, created a program where kids from the city wrote letters back and forth with kids on-reserve. Simple, and profoundly important. They got to know each other.

The last thing is to extend the intention of fostering healthy relationships beyond people to consider a relationship with the land itself. An amazing acknowledgement I heard a year ago listed, in point form, gifts the land had provided. It went on to say that while we can't offer the land much (the land would be better off without us, to be frank), we can take better care of it, and we can thank it for what it provides. A nice, finishing touch is to use a word from the language of one of your Indigenous neighbours. For Cree people, the word for *thank you* is *ekosani*. Learning a few words in somebody else's language is a show of respect. When you're done, you'll have a statement that not only acknowledges the land but carries an intention to build relationships that will help us move forward together in a good way.

Here's an example of a great land acknowledgement, to give you a reference.

In the spirit of Truth and Reconciliation and as Treaty people, we would like to acknowledge and recognize that our meeting today takes place on the traditional lands of the Treaty 3 Anishinaabe people. We also recognize that the students and families we learn and work with at our schools extend to lands beyond Treaty 3 into Treaty 5 and Treaty 9 territories and so we honour those lands and relationships with the Anishinaabe peoples as well.

. . . As students representing classes across our board, we are grateful to the land for many reasons:

- We are grateful for the outdoor learning environment many of our school grounds provide;
- We are grateful for the trees and rocks that we can build forts with;
- We are grateful for the hills that we can slide down in the winter;
- We are grateful for the fields we have to play soccer, baseball, and tag on;
- We understand that the land gives us all of this and it is our responsibility to help take care of this land.

Please take a moment now to acknowledge what this land gives to you and how you can honour it. Thank you.

That acknowledgement was written by Shannon Elliott's students in the Keewatin-Patricia District School Board, which serves communities in Northwestern Ontario. First of all, great job to Shannon and the many teachers doing work like this in the classroom. Second, we can learn a lot from kids. Once you've written your acknowledgement, go ahead and share it, and encourage others to do the same.

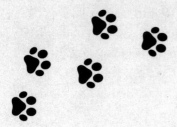

Week #7

CHECK YOUR IDIOMS

FILE THIS ONE under decolonizing the way we speak. Let's try to be mindful of the words we use, because some of the idioms in our everyday vocabulary can be at best offensive, and at worst racist, whether it's unintentional or not. Typically, I think the best of people, and so I'd like to think that in almost every instance of an idiom being used that involves Indigenous people, our culture, or our ceremonies, the person saying it doesn't think it's offensive. Even the possibility that it could be may not enter their mind. Either way, though, it is harmful, and I want to make you aware of it, and in so doing, help steer your idiom vocabulary in a different and better direction.

"Let's have a powwow!" Typically, that does not mean somebody has had the bright idea to literally put on a powwow; it means that the speaker wants to have a meeting, usually in a business setting. Using that idiom as an example probably seems too obvious. Not to assume (I don't like assuming), but

I'm guessing that most people reading this, when presented with the saying, are keenly aware of why it may be offensive or problematic. But when a saying like this is so pervasive, that awareness may not matter. The words can slip into our conversations without us noticing; it's perfunctory. I was on a virtual call a couple of years back, post-pandemic. The call was to do with one of my books, and when the meeting came to an end and it was clear that more conversations were needed, one of the attendees used that exact phrase when planning a subsequent meeting. "Let's get back together and have a powwow," they started. Before I was able to point it out, because I try to make a habit of doing so when I feel it's appropriate, another non-Indigenous person on the call did it for me, which meant a lot.

I understand that it's hard to immediately shift the way we do things or say things. It takes time. But having an awareness of what is appropriate and what is not equips us to integrate changes in our vocabulary. It just takes a bit of intentionality. So much of this comes down to intention. Not only the topic of idioms but almost everything I'm writing about in this book. You must have an intention in whatever it is you do. It'll make what you do so much more effective. If you catch yourself saying "Let's have a powwow," just correct yourself. Again, we all make mistakes. "Let's meet about this another time" is an easy substitute. "Let's get back together." The good thing is that an idiom is just another way of saying something. With that logic, just say it a different way.

A good activity is to list some of the idioms you can think of that are potentially offensive—either because they're racist, or because they trivialize cultural practices or ceremonies. On social media, just the other day, somebody sent out a post that stated simply that a celebrity was their spirit animal. That phrase is both problematic and inaccurate. It does reference

Indigenous people, of course. There is a misconception that *spirit animal* refers to something Indigenous people have. Anybody who knows me knows that I love bears. Bears are not my spirit animal, however. I do not know of any Indigenous cultures that use the term *spirit animal*. Yes, Indigenous people have a strong spiritual connection to the water, land, and nature, including animals, fish, and birds, but that does not make one of them a spirit animal. My father told me that the bear is our relative. So, our family has a strong connection to the bear. We may not hunt bears as a result, but the bear is not my spirit animal. Once more, all this phrase does is trivialize meaningful aspects of Indigenous cultures and our spirituality. Instead of thinking that Taylor Swift is your spirit animal, maybe you can call her your muse, kindred spirit, or patronus (if you want to use a fantasy-like term). Because our cultures are not the stuff of fantasy, in the same way that our traditional clothing is not a costume.

Circle the wagons. Low man on the totem pole. Indian Summer. Indian Time. Too many Chiefs and not enough Indians. That's one my son heard recently in the dressing room of a hockey team he played for. He was not happy about it and handled it in a good way with the person who uttered the phrase. And that's the thing to really internalize. If you're going to be an ally, you have to be prepared to have hard conversations. Those conversations have to include pointing out to others when you hear something that you know is not accurate or right. And so, when somebody says "Low man on the totem pole," you ought to speak up about it. Of course, you first have to know why it's not accurate (totem poles, which belong to the Indigenous Peoples in the Northwest Pacific, do not have a hierarchy of carvings based on physical position), and once you do, you can respectfully notify somebody of what they said, and that they can say it differently.

What they do from there is out of your hands, but rest assured, you've taken a small but important action.

I was at a writer's festival earlier this year, somewhere in Canada, watching a panel about the publishing industry and how to break into it. After the panel, an audience member asked, "How do I find my tribe?" What he meant was, how would he go about finding other writers to form a group with? I texted a friend of mine, another writer who was in the audience, something like, "If nobody says anything, I'm going to lose it." Not only did nobody say anything, but somebody on the panel repeated the phrase. Crickets. In that case, I chose not to speak up because I wanted to see if somebody else would. Silence is not an answer. Silence is not allyship. Reconciliation means that we shoulder the burden of change together, and do not leave the weight on the shoulders of Indigenous people. It's not helping us to walk but walking with us. It is completely your place to say something if you know what's been said is not right. Do not be complacent; be active and be informed.

And by the way, I'm always early to everything. So put that in your pipe and smoke it.

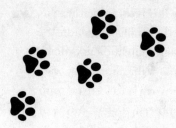

START A SECOND BOOK IN YOUR INDIGENOUS BOOK CLUB

MY MAIN CONCERN is that we don't make the book club a "one and done" kind of thing, where one book is read, and we may feel as though we've done enough and move on to read other literature. Truthfully, I don't think that'll happen, because we tend to write good stories, but encouraging the continuation of your Indigenous storytelling immersion is part of the reason why I'm here. I've the same concern with the National Day for Truth and Reconciliation—that we pay attention to important issues and history for the day, and then go on about our lives until next September 30.

All this being said, it's time for a second book in the Indigenous book club. I'm going to offer a bit of direction here, but you are by no means bound to it. There are robust sections in bookstores now that are dedicated to Indigenous books, and finding one that interests you and that you feel would be of benefit to your group of readers is most important. A story that can be enjoyed but that also educates in some way. Over the last several years in the publishing industry, you have seen a growing and rich collection of Indigenous non-fiction literature, in particular in the area of memoirs. If we're talking about reconciliation, and we agree that the definition of reconciliation has something to do with learning through storytelling, through learning about another person's lived experience, what better way to approach this than by reading a memoir?

What I find hard to do is to pinpoint only one, because there are many I've read that are beautiful, excellent, and powerful. If you believe that books are mirrors, windows, and sliding glass doors, a concept articulated by Dr. Rudine Sims Bishop, memoirs by Indigenous authors are the sliding glass doors; they welcome you in, to experience life through somebody else's eyes. Walking in another person's moccasins, to use a strained, albeit fun twist on the traditional idiom. There are many worth reading, as they directly address a survivor's or intergenerational survivor's experience with the Indian Residential School System. Works like *Broken Circle* (Theodore Niizhotay Fontaine), *The Reason You Walk* (Wab Kinew), *The Education of Augie Merasty* (Joseph Auguste Merasty with David Carpenter), or *In My Own Moccasins* (Helen Knott) are vital, and excellent selections for any book club. If you wanted to, you might even check out a memoir by yours truly, entitled *Black Water*, which addresses the Indian Residential School System, but also colonialism, intergenerational trauma, and healing through reconnection to land, culture, and family.

All I'm going to do is throw out a couple of other options, and then you can head over to your local indie bookstore and pick the one that is of most interest to you. *From the Ashes* by Jesse Thistle is an incredible story of resilience, as Thistle's journey brings him from addiction and homelessness back to family, community, and higher education. *A Mind Spread Out on the Ground* by Alicia Elliott is a collection of personal essays that deal explicitly and powerfully with mental health and intergenerational trauma. *"Indian" in the Cabinet* was Jody Wilson-Raybould's first work of non-fiction; it deals with her experience in politics as a highly talented and accomplished Indigenous woman. *Mamaskatch* by Darrel J. McLeod was a Governor General's Literary Award winner and deservedly so, as it delves deep into his coming of age in a uniquely structured narrative. And finally, but not least, and not the last memoir available to seek out and buy, there's one of the first books I can remember by an Indigenous author: *Halfbreed* by Maria Campbell, an iconic book in Canadian literature that details, unflinchingly, the experience of a Métis woman living in this country and its colonial history.

Those are some options for you, but this list is, as is this case with other lists I've included in this book, not exhaustive. Part of the experience is looking for the right book, spending time with each option, reading about it, and feeling which one might resonate with you most. What I have found with memoir is that even though we may be from different backgrounds, we share a lot as human beings, and finding those connections is not only healing but, within the context of reconciliation, an important step on the journey. I think often we are able to insulate ourselves from the difficult experiences and events in history because it may not directly involve us. But we need those intimate connections to feel accountable to one another, to understand powerfully and meaningfully that we are walking together. We could all do with getting to know each other better, no matter your background or lived experience.

Memoir brings the reader into the author's life. It is an invitation that I hope you accept, and that impacts you profoundly.

Week #9

SUPPORT AN INDIGENOUS MUSICIAN

I'M PARTIAL TO this one. Music has played a huge role in my life as a writer and as an Indigenous person. The same is true for Indigenous musicians as is true for Indigenous writers, and artists generally. Not only are we good at what we do, but there is an incredible diversity in what we do. For example, Indigenous writers don't stick to only comics, picture books, or novels. We do it all. And not only do we write novels, we write in all genres. Indigenous musicians dip their toes into all types of genres as well. That's exciting, and since they are storytellers who have a wide reach, it's vital.

When I was a young, up-and-coming writer, still not in a place where I felt as though I even belonged, I was given the opportunity to be the writer-in-residence for Aqua Books, a cultural hub in downtown Winnipeg that has since gone out of business. This was around 2008, and it was the craziest thing. Not only was I an actual writer, but I had an office in the shop, and I got to plan events for the public. My friend Niigaan Sinclair and I planned a series that showcased Indigenous artists—writers and at least one musician.

It was one of the coolest moments when the icon Beatrice Mosionier, author of *In Search of April Raintree*, left a new, young musician named William Prince starstruck. Back then, William Prince was fresh-faced and playing one of his first public gigs. Everybody knew he was incredibly talented— that was clear from the first note—but it's gigs like that, where people come out to support an artist, that make artists believe they can make their dreams come true. I'm still friends with William, but I won't speak for him. From personal experience, I know the impact it had on me to have an event where a bunch of people showed up. I remember saying to myself, standing at the front of the Prairie Ink Restaurant at McNally Robinson Booksellers, "I can do this."

William Prince happens to be one of my favourite Indigenous musicians, even today. Strike that. He's one of my favourite musicians. It just so happens that he's Indigenous. But in being Indigenous, he has a perspective and gravitas that has helped make him truly special. His music is skillful, his voice is out of this world, but his lyrics put him over the top in the stories that he weaves together. Where is he today? He's a Juno Award–winning artist who has opened for Willie Nelson. I am sure that he, as much as any other artist, Indigenous or otherwise, is intimately aware that he would not be where he is today without the people who have supported his music. Bought tickets to his concerts. Paid to download and listen to his songs while they drive, work out, or go for a walk. Where would I be without readers? It's the same thing.

Of course, William Prince is one of many Indigenous musicians working today. We talk a lot about healing when we consider reconciliation, and music is medicine. That's how I have always felt. When I was having a tough year, in 2020 and 2021, as many people were, certain things helped me through that hard time, and one of them was music. All music, but the work of Indigenous musicians was a balm. Whatever kind of music you're into, I guarantee you there is an Indigenous artist who does it well. If you like country or folk, there is Don Amero, Crystal Shawanda, or Susan Aglukark. If you like electronic music, there are few better than the Halluci Nation, formerly known as A Tribe Called Red. Rock? Punk? There's Blackfire or Digging Roots. If you want somebody who gives you a bit of everything, from hip-hop to electronic to jazz, there's iskwē. And there is a huge pool of talent in rap/hip-hop across Turtle Island. As with the world of writing, there are too many people to mention, but, as always, doing a bit of research will give you a wealth of artists and bands to choose from. And, as with writing, I'd also encourage you to try new genres and step out of your comfort zone. Music from Tanya Tagaq and Jeremy Dutcher is beautiful, challenging, inspiring, and often blends the traditional with contemporary, to startling effect.

Aside from seeking out and supporting individual artists by watching their music videos, following them on social media, attending their concerts, and downloading their music, there are organizations that can be supported as well that are focused on promoting and developing Indigenous talent. A local organization in Manitoba is called Indigenous Music. Its mission is "to support First Nation, Métis, and Inuit artists and music companies as they build sustainable careers in Manitoba's music industry. The program delivers projects and services that respond to the needs of the industry as identified by a steering committee." They not only have programs for artists, but also maintain a database of artists that you can use as a guide to seek out new music that will enrich, entertain, and often educate.

We need more storytellers. The more support we provide, the better opportunities for new, emerging, and established musicians to do their work, pursue their dreams, and spread their message. As always, because learning, or in this case, listening, isn't ever quite enough, make sure you tell others when you find somebody, or a band, that you really like. There are easy ways to share on different music streaming sites, or directly with a friend if you want them to check out a particular song. Or why not do it old-school? I don't necessarily mean making a mix tape like we used to do in the 1980s and 1990s, but blasting music for other people to hear is a way to present a piece of art to others; making a playlist public for other people to listen to is also effective. It's no different than lending somebody a book, and can have a profound impact on an artist.

Week #10

SUPPORT THE RENAMING OF COLONIAL MEMORIALIZATIONS

YOU MAY HAVE seen it on the news, heard people talk about it around the water cooler, or read it somewhere. Bolstered by the "discovery" of unmarked graves in Canada at former Indian Residential School sites, there has been a coinciding movement to rename streets and buildings that memorialize people who were instrumental in colonial history generally, and in the development of the Indian Residential School System (IRSS) specifically. These are often household names, and if they are not, we drive down streets named after them, or our children go to schools named after them, without giving it much, if any, consideration.

But we should.

Let's look at a couple, just to provide much-needed context to the conversation. The first person that comes to mind is a man by the name of Egerton Ryerson. In Winnipeg, there was a school named Ryerson Elementary, in Toronto, Ryerson University, and I'm sure that there are other streets or buildings named after the man in Canada. So, who was Egerton Ryerson? At a glance, he accomplished a lot. He was known mostly as an educator, serving as superintendent of education in Canada West, where he established a system of free primary and secondary-level education. He has a list of other impressive accomplishments as well. But here's the thing. In working towards free and mandatory education, he also advocated different systems of education for Indigenous people. He wanted a system of education for Indigenous children that would convert them to Christianity—he was a minister—and assimilate them into Euro-Canadian society. And that means exactly what you think it does: he was involved in the creation of the IRSS in Canada.

Bishop Grandin, the namesake of Bishop Grandin Boulevard in Winnipeg, was a Roman Catholic priest who was an early supporter of the IRSS. He believed that Indigenous people faced extinction and the only hope for them was to become civilized. It's very much a "white saviour" thing. Grandin is quoted as saying, in 1875, that the goal of the schools is to "instill in them a pronounced distaste for the native life so that they will be humiliated when reminded of their origin. When they graduate from our institutions, the children have lost everything Native except their blood."

Of course, there were more people involved in the development and implementation of the IRSS, many of whom, just like Grandin and Ryerson, have been memorialized. But the grandfather of it all, the architect of the system, was John A. Macdonald, the first prime minister of Canada—which is, without question, an enormous achievement. The figurehead of the Canadian Confederation and a significant force in politics for almost half a century. Unfortunately, Macdonald has a checkered and problematic historical track record. Not only was he the man directly responsible for the IRSS, but he was, for good measure, involved in the North-West Resistance and the hanging of Louis Riel, and played a role in the Chinese Head Tax, a fixed fee charged to each Chinese person entering Canada starting in 1885, nine years after the Indian Act came into being.

Here's the thing. There's been significant debate over the renaming of schools, buildings, and streets. The detractors of the movement to strip away these memorializations will say that it's erasing history and that keeping these things in place, including statues, which have been toppled in recent years all over Canada, is important. It reminds us of our history, and maybe prompts conversations over somebody like Macdonald's accomplishments and failures. But memorializing isn't documenting history. Memorializing is honouring somebody or something and preserving it in a good way. I say *in a good way* because you don't see a memorial in place that preserves problematic historical figures.

I went on a trip to Germany in 2023, and while I was there, I asked one of the people I spent time with on a tour of several cities if there were any streets, buildings, or statues in place to memorialize architects of the Holocaust. I knew the answer, and I'm sure you do as well. They very quickly said, "No, of course not." In fact, in Germany, it's illegal to name your child after one of the worst human beings in the history of this planet. In Canada? The scales are different. Six million people were not exterminated. But if somebody was, in part, responsible for the development of a system, the IRSS, that took in approximately 150,000 children, and that, directly or indirectly, led to the deaths of around 10 percent of those children, would you want to memorialize them? I don't think so, but that's exactly what has happened in Canada. It's ironic that for decades we ignored the history but, at the same time, honoured the people responsible for it.

History is immutable, no matter how hard some try to change or ignore it. My father always used to say that what happened happened, and we cannot go back and change it. Taking down a statue or changing the name of a school or a street is not history erasure; quite the opposite, it shows an understanding and acknowledgement of history, and it shows respect to those who may be triggered by having to drive down a street named after a person who was one of the architects of a system responsible for trauma that may very well live in their family, in their community, in their own life.

After the news of unmarked graves spread across Canada, change started to happen. Bishop Grandin Boulevard in Winnipeg has since been renamed, despite some opposition, to Abinojii Mikanah, an Anishinaabe phrase that means "Children's Way." Public pressure led to the city council making the motion, citing a re-evaluation of Grandin's legacy. I would think the question was, "Do we really want to honour this man?" Rather, they opted to honour the children. Apropos, Ryerson University is now Toronto Metropolitan University, and it was students who led the charge to rename Ryerson Elementary School. They were successful. I've spoken at the newly named Prairie Sunrise School in Winnipeg, and I cannot tell you how special that visit was. I speak often about how youth are leading the way, and I, as well as you, can follow suit. Are there memorializations in your area that are begging for a re-examination, given the information we now have related to Canada's colonial history? If so, contact the appropriate government representative (and have others do the same) to ask about changing the name so that we honour the right people, in the right way, and keep history where it belongs, and where it is *not* erased: in textbooks, in the classroom, where educators can provide proper context. Yes, this person accomplished these things, but they were also responsible for this, and let's have a conversation about it.

Week #11

LEARN EVERYDAY WORDS IN INDIGENOUS LANGUAGES

I TOUCHED ON the importance of language previously. I do this wherever I go, and in speaking about land acknowledgements, I mentioned how important it was as a part of the development of your own land acknowledgement to learn some words in an Indigenous language. I want to expand on that a little bit because I don't see many issues as important as language revitalization; it's right up there with environmental protection. Elders will tell you—my father said many times—that if you lose the language, you lose the culture. Despite the work that is being done in many Indigenous communities to keep the language vibrant, at times it feels like a losing battle. The speakers are getting older, and without them to teach the young ones, there are fewer people to learn from. As a result of this reality, you might say that the government and the church did an effective job, over the long term, but I think there's hope and, like almost every other act of reconciliation, everybody can play a part in some way.

There is nothing to say that you can't learn and become fluent in an Indigenous language, but a good starting point is to acknowledge what a meaningful sign of respect it is to make an effort to learn keywords. As with anything else, you have to lay a foundation if you're going to build something sturdy. I think this is cross-cultural, too. Last year, I had the opportunity to travel overseas for the first time, to Hong Kong and Germany. Now, when I go to Montreal or Quebec City, which I do usually once a year, I know enough to be able to say "thank you" and "hello" and maybe a few other phrases in French. They quickly change to English because they recognize that I don't speak, but I like to think that they appreciate the effort. I tried to do the same in Hong Kong and Germany. I learned how to greet people, thank people, and say a few short phrases during my trips, but I also came away with more knowledge each time. For example, in Germany, I didn't know that how you say hello to somebody differs depending on what region you are in. I asked questions and found out some of the history that explains the geographic nuances that exist in the German language.

And that's the first point: it's not that you should learn a few words in an Indigenous language; it's that you need to learn a few words that are appropriate and that are linked to Indigenous communities close to where you live. In Canada, there are more than seventy Indigenous languages that are spoken by different Indigenous cultural groups, and while you don't have to learn words in all seventy, you have to make sure you are learning words from the right one (or the right ones; there are often a couple of Indigenous groups in close proximity to each other—from where I live, you can drive for around two hours and hit a Dakota community, an Anishinaabe community, and a Cree community [Fisher River Cree Nation and Peguis First Nation are neighbours]).

I made the mistake of not knowing words from the right language years ago, when I was first learning more about Indigenous communities and my identity as a Cree man, and I did it in front of several hundred people. It was at the book launch for my first graphic novel, *The Life of Helen Betty Osborne*, which was independently published in partnership with the Helen Betty Osborne Memorial Foundation. The launch was during their annual gala, a fundraising event, as the foundation is in place to assist Indigenous students in achieving post-secondary education. Murray Sinclair, my cousin via traditional adoption, introduced me and the work, which was appropriate, as he was one of the chairs of the Aboriginal Justice Inquiry. He was eloquent, as always, and then it was my turn. I think I did a pretty good job, considering how nervous I was. My parents were there. I'd attended the galas before with them; my father had a strong connection to the foundation. After I finished, I looked over the crowd and thanked them in what I thought was the right language. "Meegwetch," I said. Following the gala, at the book signing in the hall outside the event, my father told me quietly that we were Cree, and that *meegwetch* was an Anishinaabe word. I should've said "Ekosani." I made a mistake but learned an important lesson, and since that time, I've said thank you in Cree because that's my heritage on Dad's side. In Winnipeg, you can't go wrong saying thank you in either language, and a couple more. What I would do is specify what language you are using so that people can receive a very brief education, whether you're speaking in front of hundreds of people or just saying thanks to somebody one-on-one. If you visit a local Indigenous community, you want to make sure you're using the proper language.

Here's the second part. Where do you learn the words from? There are a few options. If you search online, it's relatively easy to find tools that will help you translate words into the appropriate language (and appropriate dialect). When I'm stuck and looking for a word, I tend to use creedictionary.com, which translates words into various dialects and also provides the translations in syllabics. What I make sure to do after finding the translation is cross-reference it in some way, either by asking a speaker or referring to one of the few Cree dictionaries my father gave me. I try not to get too stressed about the spelling, just that the word is right; there are various ways to spell, and no standard way, for the Cree language. My father used to spell words phonetically. Depending on the language, there may be an app available for your phone that will help you translate words and phrases. I know there are a couple for Anishinaabemowin and Cree, and there are certainly a couple for other Indigenous languages as well. Call me old-school (I am probably literally old-school now, at my age), but I think the best resources are between the pages of a book. It could be a dictionary, a work of creative writing (I incorporate the Cree language in every novel I write now), a picture book that helps you learn how to count to ten, or a book that has been translated entirely into an Indigenous language (something creative and overtly developed for the purposes of language revitalization). *When We Were Alone*, for example, is available entirely in Swampy Cree, with the English words at the bottom for reference.

I can think of a few Indigenous language books off the top of my head, but if you visit your local indie bookstore or Indigo, or order from an Indigenous-run business like GoodMinds, they are not hard to find, and they're almost always colourful, engaging, and fun to read, especially if you're a parent reading with your child (or a teacher reading with your students). But even if you don't have kids, picture books that teach Indigenous languages are a useful resource to learn a few words, or a few numbers, that you can put into practice as a sign of understanding, respect, and community.

Week #12

SUPPORT INDIGENOUS ATHLETES

A FEW YEARS AGO, my son had the honour of representing Team Manitoba at the National Aboriginal Hockey Championships (NAHC), both in 2022 and 2023. In 2023, the Manitoba boys won gold, and the girls won silver. The tournament was in Winnipeg, which made the victory even sweeter. The previous year, in 2022, the tournament was in Membertou, Nova Scotia, where Team Ontario and Team Manitoba were the gold-medal winners for the boys and girls, respectively. My wife went to that tournament, and I watched the games online.

I went to almost all the games in Winnipeg, at Seven Oaks Arena, a beautiful facility in the Garden City area. What I noticed in attending the games in person was that it was more than just a celebration of hockey and sportsmanship and everything great about hockey; it was a celebration of Indigenous cultures. I heard many jokes, funny jokes, about how Seven Oaks Arena turned into an urban reserve for the week. It's true; there were a lot of Indigenous folks packing the stands. But there were a lot of other people from different cultural backgrounds, too. And that was amazing to see.

Being a hockey parent, I've seen and heard of many incidents of racism in hockey. If we're talking about culture, we should mention the culture of hockey. It can have a bad rep. Some of that is warranted. Indigenous hockey players, as well as Black hockey players and people from the LGBTQIA2S+ community, face more than just on-ice challenges. They should be able to just play the game, and they often can't. They have to hear people from the stands yelling at them, or opposing players chiding them, and a hundred other things thrown their way.

Here's the thing. I really believe that these attitudes come from a small number of people with loud voices. I've been to enough places in Canada and met enough people to know that the majority of people in this country are great. Yes, there needs to be a culture shift in the sport of hockey, but if you look, and sometimes not even that hard, you can see things that give you hope. At the NAHC, there was a whole bunch of hope. The stands were packed, the arena was packed, and everybody that I saw was cheering on all the kids working their asses off to win a medal. It didn't matter if the fans were Indigenous or white, male or female, tall or short . . . it was an incredible display of sportsmanship from fans and an appreciation not only of effort and a great sport but of the many cultures that had gathered together in an arena in the northern part of the city. I remember watching the stands as my son's team was seconds away from winning gold, thinking, *This is what sport is all about.*

Just this past week, I was doing school visits in North Dakota, in a small town called Bottineau, where the boys' team is still called the Braves and has an Indigenous mascot (it takes time to change—I had a great conversation with a teacher about how maybe one day the name will be different), and the girls' team is called the Stars. At one point, however, they were called the Squaws. That's just as bad as the Washington Commanders' old moniker. So, there was a really good thing, and there was a bit of work to be done. And people, for the most part, recognized that. What's my point? When I go to another city or town to spend some time, I like to do more than just present to classes. I like to get to know the community a little bit. It's a genuine interest. That's how the conversation about mascots happened. We were just talking about the town, not books. I was there for two days, and on the first day, in the evening, instead of chilling out in the hotel room, I went to a basketball game and a hockey game. The high-school girls, the Stars, were ranked second in the state at the time and were the favourites heading into their game at the school, while the high-school boys, the Braves, were playing Minot, a relative juggernaut that some of the kids, that day, didn't feel too confident playing against (they put up a great fight, by the way, losing 4–1 including an empty net goal). The Stars played a team that had a large number of Indigenous players, and even though we were in a small town in the United States, the cheers for them were just as loud. There was applause coming from both sides of the stands to appreciate good plays (of course, they had their own enthusiastic cheering section).

And it's a matter of perspective. You can choose to see that a team still has an outdated and potentially offensive mascot, or you can choose to hear the applause in the stands for talented Indigenous players.

Supporting Indigenous athletes, Indigenous teams, and Indigenous tournaments ensures that Indigenous athletes can continue to play, participate, and draw crowds from all walks of life. I can't imagine how amazing, empowering, and cathartic it was for the kids on the ice during the gold-medal ceremony in Seven Oaks Arena to see a crowd full of fans cheering them on. It's pretty much the polar opposite of the remarks from ignorant people that can tear a kid down and convince them not to play a sport that might be one of their only outlets to escape from the hard things that Indigenous children have to live through, that other kids do not.

It's more than that. Reconciliation is also about the bonds we form as Indigenous people and the healing that comes from those bonds. It's like I've said on many occasions, and probably more than a few times in this book: reconciliation includes healing within communities and between communities, on an individual scale, or a bigger scale. When my daughter swam for Team Manitoba at the North American Indigenous Games (NAIG), she had the time of her life. She was representing her province, her people—Cree and Métis—winning medals and feeling great about herself, but she was also forming bonds with swimmers and athletes from other areas of Turtle Island. She came home with pins from friends she'd made, some of whom she continued to talk to long after the games ended. And just like at the NAHC, NAIG saw a wide demographic of people cheering on athletes competing at a high level against each other, but also, in a way, for each other.

Sometimes I think back on the early years of the 2000s when I trained to play for Team Manitoba in basketball when NAIG was in Winnipeg. I was on a team playing against a high-powered group of ex-university players, competing for the chance to represent Manitoba. We almost pulled off a huge upset, but Kevin Chief, my friend (who just happened to be playing with the other team), threw a couple of darts late in the game to seal a victory, as Kevin Chief tended to do during his playing days. But even then, after the game, all the players from both sides of the court shook hands and congratulated each other amidst a chorus of cheers from supportive fans. I guess it was good enough. When I see people who played in that game, we still talk about it.

Long story short, I've got an activity for you that you may have to wait for, depending on what's going on in your area during the year. Find a sport, find a team, find a tournament that is mostly, if not all, Indigenous, and go cheer them on. It's something I've suggested you do, but because of everything I've mentioned, I have a feeling that by the end of the game, you'll be cheering because you want to, because you'll see the joy on the athletes' faces, the pride, the camaraderie, the appreciation, the sense of community, as thick and ubiquitous as thunderous applause, or the smell of popcorn in an arena lobby.

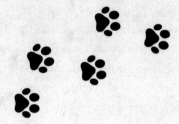

EDUCATE YOURSELF
ABOUT THE SIXTIES SCOOP

CANADA, AND IN some instances the church, has a long history of taking children, as well as adults, from their families and communities. Knowing this is a prerequisite if we are to grasp the scope of trauma that has been levelled on Indigenous people, and the resultant healing that is required. You don't have to look far to see various examples. For instance, on the east coast of Canada, there were the Beothuk, or, according to European settlers, "the Red Indians," due to the masks of ochre they painted on their faces. The Beothuk were likely kidnapped and taken overseas by settlers as early as the 1500s, which would make them the first Indigenous people to be showcased in Europe as if they were attractions at a circus. Onlookers were charged to see these exotic-looking people, often children. Their apprehension, along with other factors, such as cutting off their access to food sources, resulted in their extinction by the mid-1800s. The last known Beothuk, Shawnadithit, died of tuberculosis in 1829. More on the Beothuk later.

Of course, there was the Indian Residential School System (IRSS), where Indigenous children were taken at will by the church and the Canadian government; the kidnapping of Indigenous children was literally mandated by Canada starting in 1884, and this policy remained in place until 1951, when the Indian Act was repealed and replaced with a different version, which no longer made it mandatory for Indigenous children to attend a residential school (though in many cases it was the only option if an Indigenous child was to receive secondary education). During the time that it was mandatory for Indigenous children to attend residential schools, parents who tried to keep their children away from the horrors they were well aware of, many of whom having attended themselves, could be fined or imprisoned.

The last residential school closed in 1997, Kivalliq Hall in Rankin Inlet, and with that closure, you might think *That's it, we're good*, but that's not the case at all. There was, and remains, the foster care system, which many Indigenous communities rightfully think of as a second residential school system. Why? Stop me if you've heard this one. The foster care system apprehends children and takes them away from their families and communities. In doing so, they are ostensibly removed from culture, language, ceremonies, beliefs, values, traditions, and histories, unless you've got a set of really good foster parents who can work to maintain meaningful contact so an Indigenous child does not lose a huge piece of their identity. Not *all* children in foster care are Indigenous, but the *majority* of kids in foster care are. Statistics Canada released numbers in 2021 that said 53.8 percent of kids in care were Indigenous, while accounting for only 7.7 percent of the population of children. That's almost exactly seven times higher than the percent of the population of children in Canada. That's an awful, and concerning, if not disturbing, disparity.

So, you definitely need to learn about the contemporary issues related to the foster care system in Canada. It speaks to how today, families and communities are still experiencing trauma, that the struggles of the past are, often, the struggles of today. We cannot reconcile if we're doing the same things we have done in the past. And there are more Indigenous children in foster care today than at the peak of the IRSS.

But that's the tip of the iceberg. In the not-so-distant past, Indigenous children and families were unwilling participants in what a researcher named Patrick Johnston called the "Sixties Scoop," where Indigenous children were "scooped" by the Canadian government and placed into the welfare system at a massive rate. The Sixties Scoop took place between 1951 and the 1980s, a period that saw Indigenous children adopted by non-Indigenous families in Canada and the United States. Child welfare in Canada is in place to protect children's health and well-being, and it should come as no surprise that Indigenous families have been historically targeted. The fact is that poverty is rampant on reserves, along with high death rates, substance abuse, and many other struggles. All of this provides a good excuse to take children away. I mean, we're protecting them, right?

Not exactly. Taking children away from a difficult situation does not address the root problem. What it does is encourage the continuation of a cycle of trauma. And these struggles are almost universally a result of colonization. How does it make sense that the government gives itself the authority to take children away to protect them from a problem the government created? Parents, very often, did not agree with their children being taken away. They likely were aware, as you should be, that the Sixties Scoop and the foster care system in general were not in place to protect children from bad parents but rather continued attempts by the government to assimilate Indigenous Peoples. As usual, the government is quite clever in making children the targets of assimilation.

It has been acknowledged now, even though problems persist, that the Sixties Scoop, along with the IRSS, was part of a cultural genocide. To better understand the system and its impacts on Indigenous children, parents, families, and communities, take some time to research the system at large, and the Sixties Scoop specifically, to develop an articulate and broad understanding. Along with many systems in Canada's past and present, it's a piece of a large puzzle, and learning about it helps to fit it into place to create a full picture of why we're working towards reconciliation, and just how much it entails.

There are a number of resources out there today that will help you learn about the Sixties Scoop and the child welfare system's treatment of Indigenous people. Some of it is academic, and that can be hard to work through. But there are creative projects that have been done that can balance out what can be rather dry (albeit important) sources of information. One that I would strongly suggest, that I think every Canadian should listen to, is Connie Walker's *Missing & Murdered: Finding Cleo*. It is, hands down, the best podcast I've ever listened to, and it is an unflinching and horrifying look into the Sixties Scoop and the impact it had on one child and everybody her life touched. It not only delves deep into history, it solves a mystery, all while educating anybody who listens about a vital chapter in Canada's history.

Week #14

VOLUNTEER YOUR TIME

"THEY'RE ON INDIAN TIME."

A phrase like that is almost as commonplace as the stereotype of the savage Indian, and just as damaging. Any phrase or idiom that perpetuates a negative perception of a group of people is damaging because it sets false and unrealistic expectations for them. It's also based on a completely ignorant belief held about somebody else's way of life.

I've been subject to the term *Indian Time* myself. When I worked for an insurance corporation earlier in my life, my office (cubicle, rather) was in a building that was about a fifteen-minute walk from the YMCA-YWCA. Two of my friends and I who worked in a department of the organization used to walk over every lunch hour and work out. Well, they would work out, and I would play basketball. The games at lunch were packed and full of skilled players. I loved it. I loved it so much that I would often lose track of time, my friends

would go back to work, and I would walk back on my own, a few minutes later than I should have been. After a little while, two co-workers noticed that I was coming back late, and notified my supervisor. The phrase "Indian Time" was overheard by me, when discussing my tardiness.

It was a ridiculous statement. Sure, I rightfully got a reprimand from my supervisor for taking longer lunches (even though I skipped breaks to make up for the time), but my lateness had nothing to do with my Indigenous background; it had everything to do with basketball. I was having so much fun playing that I stayed too long. But because of the perceptions and beliefs of others, my Indigeneity was projected onto my behaviour, and voila, David was on Indian Time.

Indian Time is pretty much synonymous with the Lazy Indian stereotype. One is closely related to the other. The belief that Indigenous people are usually late is undoubtedly attributed, knowingly or unknowingly, to the "fact" that they are lazy. But it's all patently false. First of all, we're not all late all the time. My father was always early, and I am always early, too. When I have a school event, I usually arrive so early that I stay in the parking lot for a bit and wait until it's time to go in, because I don't want to get there so far ahead of schedule (or I go in early and meet the kids prior to my official visit—that's way more fun).

Whether somebody is periodically late or early depends on the situation and their personal circumstance. Living in the city, people are slaves to time. Pre-pandemic, before many people started to work remotely, the majority of those who were employed worked on the clock. Eight-hour days that started at a defined time and ended at a defined time. That's still the case in many occupations, but flex time and remote employment have changed the concept of what a working day is. Today, for example, I started working at 10:00 a.m., but I know that I'll work most of the day, off and on, and probably won't be done with all the work I have to do until this evening. I don't have a defined schedule, for the most part, but I work more than eight hours most days.

Living in a community, time is viewed differently. Working hours are circumstantial or environmental; they aren't dictated by an expected working day but rather when the work needs to be done at whatever time of day makes sense. My father used to tell me that when he lived on the land, working hours were dictated by the movement and patterns of animals and fish. If you were set on clocking in at 8:00 a.m. and clocking out at 4:00 p.m., you would likely miss the muskrat run, or when certain animals prefer to be out and about. There are other factors, of course. High rates of unemployment for various reasons, not the least of which is the availability of work, is a factor, but none of it means that time is no less important. I attend a lot of conferences, and people don't freak out when a Chief shows up late; the event starts when they arrive, and we adapt and adjust.

I think we can all agree that time is valuable. Whenever you work, wherever you work, and however you work. If you have kids, you have obligations to them that require your time and attention. If you are on a team, if you are meeting a friend for lunch, or if you want to relax in front of the television after a long day—all of that is valuable time. Life's too short to waste much of it. That's why giving your time is so meaningful, why it's a gift, because you have so many other ways to spend it.

There are a number of Indigenous organizations across Turtle Island that do important work and, at the same time, do not have the funding to pay employees to get all the work done that needs to be accomplished. They are often soft-funded and not-for-profit, and as such, they rely on the time of others through volunteerism. I've often said that on the path we're walking, there is no set way in which you can contribute; there's not one answer when somebody asks me, "What can I do to help work towards reconciliation?" Why? Because it needs to be a personal choice based on one's own journey, and people need to work within their own capacity, with whatever skills and abilities they have, to contribute. What one person does isn't necessarily what you can do, but it's all helpful, it's all meaningful, and it all makes a difference. I write books. You may play music, teach, work at the bank, or maybe you're an athlete. I don't know what you do, but I know that whatever you do, you can do something. I also know that everybody has time in their day that, as valuable as it is, they can donate to something worthwhile.

So, this week, perform a search of Indigenous organizations or events close to you, reach out to them, and find out what opportunities there are to offer your time through volunteerism. A quick search for me revealed that, locally, the sākihiwē festival welcomes volunteers. On their website, it states: "We believe that volunteering is a luxury that most Indigenous families can't afford, so we work hard to pay production assistants an hourly fee for their time. That being said, our community partners provide food handlers and event staff for each of our block parties and we encourage you to connect with them if you have the time and ability to help out." The sākihiwē festival is an annual event that runs in the summer to celebrate Indigenous music and introduce it to the city and to people who may not know just how rich and diverse our talents are in the arts. It's entertaining and educational, and putting in time to help the festival run would be a worthy choice. But there are many. As always, put in the work to find what suits you best, reach out, and find out how you can take part by giving your time. Your participation in this way would be more than welcome, and wholly appreciated.

And if you're a few minutes late to your shift, don't sweat it.

Week #15

HELP FUND
INDIGENOUS EDUCATION

WHEN MY FATHER left the reserve in the 1950s, his aspiration was to become a minister due to the influence of Christianity on the community; it was one of the first Christianized reserves in Canada and, not coincidentally, one of the earliest trading areas (often, the two go hand in hand). My father accomplished most everything he put his mind to, so of course, several years after leaving Norway House Cree Nation, he became an ordained United Church minister. I'm glad for that, not the least because he was assigned to Melita, Manitoba, where he met my mother, Bev Robertson.

Dad remained a minister his entire life and performed the odd funeral or wedding, including my brother's nuptials, later in life, after he'd stepped down from active service. But in the early 1970s, through a set of circumstances that I describe in my memoir, *Black Water*, his focus turned to Indigenous education.

For the rest of his career, his vision was to improve the quality of education for Indigenous people, both on-reserve and in the pursuit of secondary and post-secondary success.

Local control was a big concern of his. That is, simply, a community having the agency and autonomy to be able to run their own school system and develop their own curriculum that fits into their tradition, language, values, beliefs, and ways of living. Not to develop a curriculum that is beholden to a Western model of thinking and learning. An example of this is how many schools are turning back to land-based education, learning outside of an institution's four walls. That's how my father learned. On the trapline, away from even the idea of a classroom, of desks and chairs. His teachers? In the Swampy Cree dialect, he was taught many things by his parents and grandparents, and according to him, it was a good way to live, and he knew a lot. Day school didn't augment or compliment this learning; rather, it shattered the things he knew and forced him to relearn.

In order for local control to work, Indigenous educators need to be trained so that they can work in their own communities. My father developed several programs aimed at increasing the number of Indigenous teachers so that they could teach their own kids in their own communities. One of them was called BUNTEP, or the Brandon University Northern Teacher Education Program—a program that started in the 1970s and is still running today out of University College of the North, and which my father helped to implement as chair of the college's development and delivery.

The irony of teacher training programs is that, often, Indigenous people have to leave their community in order to attain post-secondary education. Helen Betty Osborne's dream was to become a teacher so that she could do the very thing my father dreamed of: teach in her own community so that other kids would not have to leave home. I worked in Indigenous education myself for many years, and I knew a handful of people who were friends with Helen Betty Osborne. Guess what? They became teachers, too.

Indigenous band members often do get financial assistance to attend post-secondary education, but there is not enough money to go around. My friend Wab Kinew once correctly stated that while people sometimes complain about how much funding Indian Affairs—now called Crown-Indigenous Relations and Northern Affairs (CIRNAC) and Indigenous Services Canada (ISC)—gets to distribute to the Indigenous population, they actually are given less than a province such as New Brunswick, even though the province has as many people as there are Indigenous people in Canada. And so, there are organizations that provide financial support to Indigenous people pursuing post-secondary education, whether they want to be teachers, doctors, engineers, writers, or anything they have a passion for. These organizations operate on government grants and public donations. It seems a complex solution, and it is, and a complex solution means complex actions are required. So what does that mean for you? How can you contribute to the improvement of access and attainment of post-secondary education for Indigenous students? Donate. Some people may be able to give more than others, but there are many ways to go about it, and giving to your capacity is perfectly fine. Every dollar counts. If you want, refer to the section on fundraising and find ways to raise money that can be donated to support Indigenous education. However you get the money, through your own personal finances or through fundraising initiatives, here are a few ideas on where your money can be of best use.

There is an incredible program called Indspire, which, among many things, includes recognizing and honouring

Indigenous people across Turtle Island who have made a difference, young and old, and provides bursaries and scholarships to Indigenous students to assist them in the attainment of post-secondary education. On their website there is a section entitled "Ways to Give," which lists different options to donate. You can make a one-time gift or contribute monthly; you can leave some money to the organization and the good work it does in your will; you can organize donations at your work (if you donate to the United Way, for example, you can stipulate that the money you donate goes to Indspire); you can even donate airline points. Another organization near and dear to my heart is the Helen Betty Osborne Memorial Foundation, established in Betty's name. It provides bursaries and scholarships annually in Manitoba to Indigenous students seeking post-secondary education.

There are many organizations that have been established in Canada, Indigenous-run organizations in particular, that have a simple goal of making sure Indigenous youth have an equal chance of being successful as youth in any other segment of the population. In a community, the success of one is the success of all, and you can contribute to that community's success this week by finding the right organization and the best way to donate to support Indigenous students in achieving higher education. I am certain that many of those students will go back home and help others do the same thing— whether it's through being a role model for other kids, who are able to see what they have done, or by working in the classroom and directly impacting the lives of Indigenous youth through culturally relevant education.

READ INDIGENOUS COMICS

I OWE A lot to comics, the reasons for which would make up an entire book, not a section within a book. I've touched on some of it here; in particular, how the historical misrepresentation or appropriation of Indigenous people and cultures that existed when I was young and hooked on comics helped me to decide that when I sought publication for the first time, it would be through graphic novels (long-form comics). But for a moment, I want to dig deeper into another reason, one that doesn't touch on the racism and stereotypes I've seen in countless comics over the years. Rather, I want to illustrate why comics are so effective, and why you should be reading them as one of your acts of reconciliation.

First, let's look at comics generally, and quickly deconstruct what they are. I do this workshop often with youth and adults. The intention is simply to provide a better understanding of what comics are, and why, when reading them with a more critical eye, they are almost the perfect tool for education.

The answers are in the images. Full credit to Gene Yang, by the way, who has done so much work in this area, and who deserves a read. I met him once at San Diego WonderCon, and it was one of the rare times I was a fanboy. Anyway. Comics are a visual medium, and that speaks to readers, young and old. Why? Well, the first form of communication was comics. Specifically, it was sequential art, of which comics are a family member, along with graphic novels, manga, and birch bark bitings, and can also be found on tapestries and ceramics and even bubble gum wrappers (ever heard of Bazooka bubble gum?). The earliest form of communication was cave paintings. These crude and beautiful illustrations were often chapters of a tribe's hunt; they told a story about the event, by putting images in sequence that told a story. If I believe in blood memory, which I do, and I recognize that it's cross-cultural, which I do, then I have to believe that the effectiveness of sequential art lies in our past, how our oldest form of communication is woven into our DNA. That makes us all, not just kids, visual learners.

But it's more than that.

There's this thing called visual permanence, a term I learned from Gene Yang, an American cartoonist. That means written stories allow readers to learn at their own pace—my daughter reads a book in two hours, and it takes me two weeks, but when reading at our pace, we learn the same. Stories that have visuals accompanying the words augment that learning by offering cues that help draw meaning from the text.

A criticism of comics and graphic novels I have heard is that they don't take as much imagination as a book, and so are less effective. Stories need to engage a person's imagination. I would argue that comics and graphic novels engage your imagination just as much as a novel does, but in a different way, and in that different way, provide us with an environment where we can absorb important teachings and engrain them more effectively than we can when reading a book without pictures. In a novel, the writer tries to create worlds that readers can lose themselves in. They paint pictures with words that conjure images in readers' minds that bring them to those places and offer them an escape, among many other things. I would never take that away from a book. I love books. But comics engage the imagination more actively. Comics are a work of sequential art. Sequential art is images in sequence that tell a story. Those images are moments in time. You cannot show every moment or else a comic would be a million pages long. What the writer and/or illustrator does is choose the best moments to put onto the page, knowing that the reader will fill in the spaces between the images. The gutters. When you read a comic next, notice how you animate the story between the pictures, to fill in those gaps. You do it unconsciously, but you do it, and as you do, you become a storyteller, just like the writer and the illustrator. As an active participant in the storytelling process, you inherently are engaged and invested in the story.

So, how does that connect to an act of reconciliation? How is the suggestion that you read a comic by an Indigenous writer relevant to healing? You can read a book about the Indian Residential School System, for example, and you will get a lot out of it, especially if there are archival photos that help to provide context to the words on the page. I can describe a residential school building to you, but seeing it is something else entirely. The brick, the institutional feel, the lack of personality or identity, the hard edges, the archaic vibe. I can describe or infer the existence of abuse (depending on the age of the reader). I can try to emulate the disconnection between identity and culture by writing about a bunch of innocent children in uniforms with their hair cut and deadness in their eyes. But there's this thing in writing called "Show, Don't Tell," and showing is always more powerful. A comic is an exercise in showing, and through that showing, bringing the reader into the world of the story. If the goal of books about, in this case, residential schools is to generate empathy and understanding of a horrific period in history, what better way to do that than to bring the reader there in as visceral a way as possible? There's no more effective way to accomplish this than by reading a comic book. (Another piece to the larger conversation is how comics encourage further reading, graduating to more complicated texts and subjects that don't necessarily have to be comic-based.)

This week, the act is simple. Read Indigenous comics and/or graphic novels. There is a growing catalogue of them in Canada. More and more incredible writers are turning to the sequential art format to tell their stories and share their truths. I've seen and read graphic novels by katherena vermette, Thomas King, Richard Van Camp, Jay Odjick, Tasha Spillett, Patti LaBoucane-Benson, Brandon Mitchell, Drew Hayden Taylor, Michael Nicoll Yahgulanaas, and more. There are graphic novels that touch on any subject you might be interested in, and stories that are published on their own or as part of an anthology. Here are a few to get you started (shamelessly, I'll include a couple of my own, but only because they're relevant).

- *7 Generations: A Plains Cree Saga* by David A. Robertson
- *Sugar Falls: A Residential School Story* by David A. Robertson
- *A Girl Called Echo Omnibus* by katherena vermette (ill. Scott B. Henderson)
- *Red: A Haida Manga* by Michael Nicoll Yahgulanaas
- *The Outside Circle* by Patti LaBoucane-Benson (ill. Kelly Mellings)
- *Borders* by Thomas King (ill. Natasha Donovan)
- *Surviving the City* by Tasha Spillett (ill. Natasha Donovan)
- *The Night Wanderer* by Drew Hayden Taylor (ill. Michael Wyatt)
- *Wendy's Revenge* by Walter Scott
- *A Blanket of Butterflies* by Richard Van Camp (ill. Scott B. Henderson)
- *This Place: 150 Years Retold* by various authors and illustrators
- *UNeducation, Vol. 1* by Jason EagleSpeaker

There are more, and a quick search will uncover a few comics and graphic novels that address almost every subject you would want to learn about, from a place of lived experience. Pick a couple, take them out of the library or buy them at your local bookstore (this, as a pleasant offshoot, supports Indigenous artists), and take a few hours to read through some vital stories, in an immersive and engaging format that will show you history, and hopefully motivate you to read and learn more.

SUPPORT AN INDIGENOUS BUSINESS

THIS IS AN easy one. There is no reading involved. Well, there's potential reading involved, depending on what business you choose to support. What *is* involved is a bit of a financial investment. It doesn't even have to be a big one. Just something that gives business to Indigenous-owned companies, or individual artists who are selling their work—beadwork, paintings, and more. If you check out a powwow, for example, there are several different options to buy Indigenous stuff, from Indigenous people.

I see a potential hesitancy. You may be concerned about cultural appropriation; there may be a thought, and it's a valid consideration, that you shouldn't be displaying Indigenous art, wearing Indigenous clothing, hanging a dreamcatcher over your bed, or putting on a pair of mukluks in the cold winter months. But that's not the case. If you're getting your Indigenous merchandise, whatever it may be, from an Indigenous artist, that's not appropriation at all. That's a good thing. You're not only likely wearing a deadly pair of moccasins, but you are also supporting Indigenous entrepreneurs, artists, and all the people who are employed by or benefit from work that comes from running a successful business.

I've talked about the issue of appropriation often, and it's something I have addressed in this guide as well. Once I've laid out what it is, we have a discussion. The endpoint of that discussion, if all goes well, is to say that we want you to buy our products and display them proudly. As a writer, I can tell you that while many Indigenous people have read my books, and I greatly appreciate that, the majority of those who've purchased my books have been non-Indigenous, and without that support, I would not be able to do what I do. I would, as I did for well over a decade, be working a second or third job so that I could keep writing. In my spare time. When the kids are in bed. Or going to a writer's festival when I'm on vacation from my job. There was a very long period of time when I didn't really take a vacation. Even when I was away with my family, I was working. Writing something or editing. I wrote *On the Trapline* while on a camping trip. This is not to say that I don't work all the time even now, but it is to say that when I am working while off on a trip at a conference or a festival, or away with family, I am not worried about work I have waiting for me at my desk at my day job. Because this is my job!

It seems as though daily there are more businesses owned or run by Indigenous people. I know that I said writing was my main job now, and it is, but I run my own publishing imprint—the only Indigenous-run publishing imprint in Canada that focuses solely on publishing Indigenous literature.

There needs to be more. I know of only one other, and it's in the United States. Cynthia Leitich Smith runs Heartdrum for HarperCollins. The fact that I'm doing it means that, in the not-so-distant future, other people will be given the opportunity. (There are Indigenous-run publishers, including Theytus, Kegedonce, Ningakwe, Pemmican, Inhabit, GDI, and others. GoodMinds publishes Indigenous authors and is also a distributor of Indigenous literature.)

Of course, we are not just in the world of literature. We, as Indigenous Peoples, have a growing presence in the world of fashion. I recently wrote about this for *Fashion* magazine. Métis artist Wenzdae Anaïs Dimaline opened her shop, Culture Coven, in March 2022, and she works with brands by people of colour and the LGBTQIA2S+ community. Lesley Hampton is an Indigenous-owned, women-led, size-inclusive clothing brand founded by Lesley Hampton in 2016. *Vogue* called it the number-one brand to keep an eye on. Locally in Winnipeg, there's Teekca's Boutique (I would be remiss not to shout-out a business that originated in my home community, Norway House Cree Nation, in 1998). Teekca's now has six locations throughout Manitoba.

Indigenous businesses can be found almost everywhere, in almost every industry. They not only provide valuable services and high-quality products, they also elevate the visibility of successful Indigenous people, smashing stereotypes such as the "Lazy Indian." Supporting them by continuing to provide your business ensures they can continue their work, and more importantly, open the door for other Indigenous people with dreams to do the work that they love. And help change this country in the process.

WATCH AN INDIGENOUS TELEVISION SHOW

I WORK IN the arts, which means I'm a part of a larger picture that extends beyond literature. It encompasses dance and music and film and television. Supporting Indigenous-created art that works to involve Indigenous people at all levels of the creative process is a simple act, but it encourages the development and involvement of the Indigenous Arts community. This is a business. If you buy a lot of books by Indigenous authors, illustrated by Indigenous illustrators, you will see, increasingly, more Indigenous books published by small and large publishing houses. Likewise, if you support the creation of, in this case, Indigenous television shows, you are, just by tuning in, contributing to raising the demand for Indigenous television. That means we are going to see more Indigenous writers, directors, producers, actors, makeup artists, camera operators, and more Indigenous people in pretty much any other job related to the creation of a television show. It's no different than what I'm trying to do in the publishing industry. I don't want there to be only more writers; I want there to be more editors, artists, graphic designers, marketers, production assistants, printers . . . and the list goes on. This, as with many things, comes down to representation.

This is probably the easiest action you can take on this path that we're walking. You get up to grab a soda (or, if you're like me, sparkling water) and some popcorn, sit on the couch, turn on the television, and pick a show from the growing list of incredible Indigenous-run television shows.

Of course, as with anything else we've been talking about, you have to make sure you're picking the appropriate show. Just like in the worlds of publishing, music, and other disciplines within the arts, there are people who may seek to profit off the growing popularity—what my buddy Richard Van Camp would call "the renaissance"—of Indigenous art.

This phenomenon is not new, but is ongoing, and fights against the positive inroads that we are trying to make as Indigenous artists. I went to Germany in 2023 and saw firsthand a great example in the character of Winnetou, who exists in books and on the screen. Winnetou is a fictional Native character in several novels by German novelist Karl May. He is, in fact, one of the bestselling German writers of all time, selling over two hundred million copies worldwide. Winnetou is a highly romanticized, inaccurately written Indigenous character that has contributed to an unhealthy fascination, in Germany, with Indigenous people. Winnetou is almost ubiquitous in the perception of Indigenous people, having appeared in approximately thirty novels (adult and children's), eleven movies, and three television series, the most recent of which came out in 2016. Please, do not watch Winnetou movies or television shows, or read Winnetou books, unless you want a crash course on how to stereotype Indigenous people.

No, what we want are television shows that entertain and educate in good ways, where stories are controlled by Indigenous people, or, at the very least, where Indigenous people have been consulted extensively in the production of documentaries, shows, miniseries, or television movies. To find out what shows accomplish this—and stop me if you've heard this one—the only work you have to do is less than an hour of research to make sure you're watching a show that is productive, not destructive. As with the Indigenous Book Club that is hopefully going strong at this point, allow me to make a couple of suggestions, just to get you started. And, once again, this is not prescriptive; it's just me giving you some ideas.

That being said, I cannot be more emphatic when I tell you that if you have not seen *Reservation Dogs* you have, so far, missed out on watching one of the best television shows of all time. And that is not hyperbole. The good thing is, since it's a streaming show, it is never too late to watch it, and it is highly binge-worthy. If you wanted to, you could watch the entire series in a day. It's so good, you might just do it, too. The first show I binged was *Lost*, with my wife. We would stay up until early in the morning watching episode after episode on DVD. After every episode ended, we would look at each other and say, "Just one more!" That's what's going to happen when you start watching *Reservation Dogs*.

What's so special about it? The show is created by Sterlin Harjo and Taika Waititi, both Indigenous. Sterlin is from the Seminole Nation of Oklahoma, while Taika is Māori. More than that, it is the first television show to feature all-Indigenous writers, directors, and an almost all-Indigenous cast and crew. Except for White Steve (you'll get it). It is a critically acclaimed series (because we make good stuff, us Indigenous people) and has received or been nominated for a number of awards. At its heart, it's about community. It's hard and brutal (the best episode of the series, and maybe one of the best TV episodes I've ever seen, is called "Deer Lady," which addresses, poignantly and brilliantly, boarding school history in the United States, and stars a national treasure, Kaniehtiio Horn), while also managing to be hilarious, and always smart. Watching the show, you get a glimpse, an authentic window, into a Native American community and the relationships that are built and fostered within it.

The show is a literal who's who of Indigenous actors, including the aforementioned Kaniehtiio Horn, Graham Greene, Gary Farmer, Sarah Podemski, Jennifer Podemski, Paulina Alexis, D'Pharaoh Woon-A-Tai, Lane Factor, Tamara Podemski, Elva Guerra, and a breakout turn by Devery Jacobs. Jacobs previously starred in the excellent *Blood Quantum*, was most recently the voice of a brand-new Indigenous superhero for the Marvel Cinematic Universe called Kahhori, and had a starring role in Marvel's *Echo*.

The success of the young actors who starred in *Reservation Dogs* is no accident. They are talented artists, and we have a wealth of them in our communities. They are socially conscious, hard-working, and doing things that a decade ago we may not have thought possible. Thanks to them and the attention they have garnered from their incredible work, not only is their potential limitless, but they have made young Indigenous kids believe they have potential, too. That anything is attainable. So keep watching, and as you do, watch, as well, as this country changes for the better. We are not taking over. Not at all. Rather, we are finally achieving a sure footing and equity in industries where we have a lot to offer for everybody.

Week #19

HONOUR AN INDIGENOUS WORLDVIEW

ORIGINALLY, I WAS going to say that you should adopt an Indigenous worldview, but it took me about five seconds to think of a different approach, because suggesting that you adopt another people's belief system feels colonial. So, I scratched that idea, backspaced the cursor, and decided that honouring an Indigenous worldview was a far better act. Adopting is choosing to take up and, in so doing, replace one worldview with another. Honouring, on the other hand, is to hold something in high regard, to look upon it with respect and admiration. You can take it on if you choose, or you can simply think of ways that the act of honouring can be carried out in your daily life (this can certainly stretch beyond one week if it resonates with you).

But what is an Indigenous worldview? There is a bit to unpack. A worldview generally is a collection of values and beliefs, attitudes, and stories about the world around certain people, which inform their lives and exist in every action they take and in every thought they have. It is a beacon. It shows us how to live a better life in the world we've entered into. Following a worldview is intended to lead us towards what is known as mino-pimatisiwin, which is Cree for "the good life." Of course, there are as many worldviews on Mother Earth as there are distinct cultures. An Indigenous worldview, then, is a worldview held by Indigenous people, but in that worldview, there is a similar intent. What makes us human, what connects us with one another, is that we all want the same thing, no matter how you define it. The good life. What we have to be careful of, always, is to not boil down an Indigenous worldview into one thing. As Indigenous people, we are not a monolith, and neither are our worldviews. There are many Indigenous cultural groups across Turtle Island, and thus many different Indigenous worldviews.

I've written in this book about how choosing something relevant in terms of geography is important—that is, if you are going to learn words in an Indigenous language, make sure it's the language of a people that live near you. In the case of honouring an Indigenous worldview, however, I don't think this applies as strongly. Buddhism, for example, originated in northeastern India sometime around the sixth century. Pretty specific. And yet, people around the world, approximately five hundred million of them, have adopted the teachings of the Buddhist religion. One of the principles of Buddhism is seeking a state above all suffering. Another is accepting four noble truths: all of human existence is suffering; the cause of that suffering is craving; the end of suffering is putting an end to that craving; and there is a path we can follow to achieve that goal. In my opinion, it doesn't matter who or where you are; those truths and the journey to achieve a state beyond suffering are a worthy pursuit. Just as in Buddhism, Christianity, Judaism, or any other worldview or religion, Indigenous worldviews have principles that lay the foundation for living a good life. Honouring those worldviews, in the context of this book on reconciliation, is living out a worldview that speaks to you for a few days and seeing how it impacts you while simultaneously honouring people who, historically, have been marginalized and the subject of cultural or overt genocide.

Of course, there are not enough pages to address all the Indigenous worldviews that exist in this country. However, I think it would be a rewarding, if time-consuming, project. While I want you to do much of the work independently, I'm going to touch on three to give you an idea of what I'm talking about. Whether you use them as an example or choose to adopt them for your action is up to you; both are perfectly fine.

HAUDENOSAUNEE GREAT LAW OF PEACE

The Six Nations Confederacy, collectively known as the Haudenosaunee, is composed of Mohawk, Onondaga, Oneida, Cayuga, Seneca, and Tuscarora people. The Great Law of Peace, dated anywhere between early in the twelfth century and 1451, was an agreement made between the five original members of the confederacy, with the Tuscarora joining later, and was articulated on a beaded belt used to tell a story or outline an agreement. These belts are known as wampum. There is a beautiful story about the origins of the Great Law of Peace, where the protagonist is Ayenwahtha (Hiawatha), a Mohawk seeking revenge on a Chief responsible for killing his family, and learning about that story from a proper source would be an important part of honouring this worldview

(Robbie Robertson, Indigenous songwriter, has a book about the legend entitled *Hiawatha and the Peacemaker*). Suffice it to say that the Great Law of Peace is a guide that leads the Haudenosaunee through all aspects of life, emphasizing the power of reason to ensure the law's three principles—Righteousness, Justice, and Health—and through those principles, instructs them how to treat others and maintain a democratic society.

THE SEVEN SACRED TEACHINGS

These are arguably the most well-known Indigenous teachings and, by extension, comprise the most well-known Indigenous worldview—so much so that the Seven Sacred Teachings may often be attributed to a blanket Indigenous worldview. I used to think it was. I remember talking about it with Dad, and he told me that the Cree teachings are different from the Seven Sacred Teachings; there are more than seven, although there is some crossover. There is a crossover with worldviews from other cultures beyond the Indigenous ways of thinking. How could there not be? There is a universality to principles such as love and respect, for example. If there isn't, there ought to be. What this means, however, is that even though honouring an Indigenous worldview is intentional, my hope is that we live out some of the core teachings in our daily lives anyway; this will just give us a frame of reference, and an opportunity to contextualize. After all, the main goal here is to connect and learn. The action this week accomplishes both inherently. The Seven Sacred Teachings are not universal to all Indigenous cultures; they originate with the Anishinaabe People and have been adopted by many (not all) Indigenous people. The teachings are love, respect, honesty, courage, truth, wisdom, and humility. On the surface, the principles seem self-evident. Take honesty. Okay. Of course, we should be honest. But there are nuances to each teaching that take time to learn and put into practice. As I have come to understand the teaching of honesty, it's not only about being honest—as in being honest to people, to not lie—but also about being honest to yourself and who you are supposed to be. How the Creator made you. That's some great nuance. I've tried to hold that teaching close because I often feel as though I need to place an avatar of myself out there in public; I just don't feel confident in my own skin. I have had to work to find the confidence to say to myself, "I'm fine the way I am; this is who I'm supposed to be, and if people don't like that, that's their issue, not mine." Respect, in relation to honesty, is project the teaching of honesty outward, to say to others, "I am okay with who you are, and I will not ask you to change because it fits into what my worldview is."

NON-INTERFERENCE

This connects beautifully to a value that exists within the Cree culture. I remember asking my father what it meant to be Cree. We were talking about how I grew up disconnected from culture, and how I wished he would have taught me how to be Cree. He asked me, in response, "How would I have taught you to be Cree? You *are* Cree." To him, the question I was circling was one about inherent identity. I was Cree, and nothing could make me more or less who I am as a Cree person. Nothing could take that away from me, and however I conducted myself was informed by my identity, and thus was reflective of my background as a Cree. But my father's insistence on not imposing an identity of what it meant to be Cree on me, ironically, was a Cree value in itself.

He explained it to me by saying that while he didn't overtly teach me how to be Cree, because you can't teach somebody something they already are, he wanted to model what it was like to live out some Cree values in how he conducted his own life. The catch was that I could either adopt what was being modelled to me, or not. The value that he spoke about most was that of non-interference; that is, you don't interfere with how another person lives. You respect and work to understand how somebody else lives, but you don't tell them that they should live one way or another.

I've tried to find a balance in how I raise my children with my wife. We try to model what it means to be a good person and to instill confidence in them in who they are as Cree/ Métis people, but we do not ever tell them they should be this thing or that thing. Who they are and who they become depends on them. Hopefully, as parents, we are giving them the tools they need to make good decisions and develop into good people. But none of it is an imposition. That connects so closely to the teaching of respect. That who somebody is is exactly who they are supposed to be, and while we can work to understand and love who somebody else is, we should not impose upon them what we want them to be. Imagine if that was how it always was. Imagine if, when colonizers arrived on Turtle Island, they met Indigenous people and thought, *You know what, they're doing just fine without us. Let's live on the same land, but we will live our way, and they can live their way.* What kind of a country would we be living in today? I can guarantee you one thing: if we'd always had that attitude, we never would have dealt with systems like the Indian Residential Schools.

There are many Indigenous worldviews, and they all have value. Research and learn about one, and live it out for a week, emulating the core values as a way of honouring who we as Indigenous people were, and are. It's a good way to learn about somebody else, and I think you will find that there is more than you think that connects us. We share a lot as human beings, including values and ways of conducting ourselves to guide us to a better way of living.

Week #20

SUPPORT INDIGENOUS TOURISM

I LEARNED THE value of Indigenous tourism in Germany, a country where Indigenous people have been romanticized and fetishized for a long time and continue to be today. I mentioned Winnetou earlier; that Germany-created fictional Native American hero is a substantial contributing factor to the problem. When I was asked to visit Germany in 2023, I saw it as an opportunity to accomplish three goals. One of them was to market my books, which have been, more and more, translated into German and published in Germany. Another goal was to do whatever I could to shift the country's perception of Indigenous people, class by class, audience by audience. I visited a number of cities over the course of a week, and each time, I tried to explain who Indigenous people really were, from our histories to our distinct cultures, to our ceremonies, right down to how we dress (which is any way we want to dress, by the way). Thirdly, my trip coincided with a big event at the Canadian embassy in Germany that celebrated Indigenous tourism in Canada.

I didn't know what to expect when I received an invite to the celebration. I try not to make assumptions because of my line of work. Making assumptions is akin to perceiving somebody or something in a certain way without a base of accurate, prior knowledge. But when I got an initial email from the public affairs officer for the Embassy of Canada, I was dubious. She wrote that Indigenous tourism was "an area of tourism gaining in profile and popularity here." From what I knew of Germany, it made sense that the concept of Indigenous tourism would be of interest there. If somebody's fascinated with something (e.g., Indigenous people), they're going to want any and all exposure to it (or, in this case, them). She asked if I'd be willing to address the potential ups and downs of this trend, and, of course, I was. I wanted to address the "trend" head-on. It was like I'd been preparing for that my entire career. I mean, I'd done so many talks about misrepresentation and stereotypes and appropriation that I felt as if I could really lean into the subject and hopefully change a lot of people's minds. My first response was, "Could you explain to me what exactly is entailed with Indigenous tourism?" I suppose I'd been able to take a breath and get some more information before reacting, which is always a good approach. Once Gudrun, the public affairs officer, responded, I realized that what I'd thought the event was going to be was not at all what was planned. I began to feel hopeful that the event would be a legitimate celebration of Indigenous cultures and a promotion of the many ways people could see the Indigenous experience first-hand—not to perpetuate stereotypes but to work towards doing away with them. The exact thing I am working towards.

When November rolled around, and I was a few days into my tour of Germany, the events at the embassy took place: a one-on-one interview with Dr. Geneviève Susemihl, an incredibly smart professor and writer, followed by an authentic showcase of the richness and diversity of Indigenous people and cultures in Canada, from coast to coast. The relatively long event seemed to pass in a second, and I stayed until things shut down. The large crowd and I were treated to Indigenous cuisine, speeches and presentations from different Indigenous people from various provinces in Canada, performances that included throat singing and hoop dancing, and a heartfelt and hilarious emcee who guided us through the evening in a good way. The whole time, I was captivated and thinking, repeatedly, *Everybody in Canada—not just in Germany—needs to be here.* This alone would help do away with so many preconceptions and unrealistic expectations, and so much ignorance towards Indigenous people and cultures.

You likely weren't at the Canadian embassy that night in Germany, but that doesn't mean you cannot experience what I and others experienced. There is a growing and vibrant tourism industry in Canada for Indigenous cultures. The goal is to provide an opportunity for Canadians and visitors to Canada to see the world through an Indigenous lens and learn so much about the Indigenous experience— ways of living, traditions, ceremonies, values, stories, land stewardship, land-based connections, cuisine . . . the stuff of reconciliation. The hub for Indigenous tourism is a website called Destination Indigenous, and from what I can tell, it's supported by and informed by Indigenous cultures. Certainly, every distinct culture at the embassy was represented by people from that culture—a vitally important detail. I've navigated through the website, and I can tell you with confidence that wherever you are in Canada, there is an experience near you that you can enjoy and learn from. An interactive map on the site shows options accessible to the public from British Columbia all the way through to Newfoundland and Labrador. If you want to see the options in list form, rather than on the map, you can scroll through tourism choices from Abenaki Aventure in Quebec, to Manito Ahbee Festival in Manitoba, to West Coast Expeditions in British Columbia, to Tutchone Tours in Yukon, to Voyageur Wilderness in Ontario, to what looks like a hundred other listings (I didn't count, but I scrolled for quite a long time).

MENTOR INDIGENOUS YOUTH

BEFORE I STARTED working in Indigenous education, I developed workforce development programs for the information and communication technologies and manufacturing industries. I also ran a feeder system at a local school in Winnipeg with a high Indigenous population that prepared youth to enter into programs that provided Indigenous students with diplomas from post-secondary institutions.

These weren't just training programs.

In the work I'd done with communities to that point, I had learned that training somebody to do a job wasn't enough when that person lived on a reserve. Life in an Indigenous community is different from life in the city. Moving from one place to another is like going to a different world. There is an element of culture shock that, if not properly addressed, inevitably leads to failure. That's why workforce development needs to go beyond job training to include transitional support to prepare for life in the city. Things like opening a bank account, budgeting money, taking the bus, and accessing resources provided by Indigenous organizations.

We provided counselling for students who needed to work through some of the struggles they had faced in their lives and what they had taken on by moving away from home. I didn't want students to have to leave home, but the reality is there aren't many jobs in communities. These vital, additional features of the program were accomplished primarily through mentorship. We trained mentors who, in turn, supported applicants. Mentorship was also a key element of youth programming. Both programs were successful, with an over 80 percent retention rate.

I attribute much of the success to mentorship. It was provided to Indigenous adults and youth. It was beneficial to them, but the mentorship experience was equally beneficial to the non-Indigenous mentors.

Becoming a mentor to Indigenous youth is a rewarding experience and a meaningful, significant part of your reconciliation journey. As a mentor, you're not only offering important support and preparation for youth to help move them in a positive direction and ensure that positive direction is sustainable. You are also building relationships that will help you to understand youth better—the gifts they have to offer, and the challenges they face that you may not have understood previously.

I suppose, in some ways, what I do, in going to classrooms and working with kids, is similar to mentorship. I have done a lot of work in Indigenous communities, and in so doing, I've learned more than I thought I would. I have seen the unique obstacles that Indigenous youth face, and that has helped me figure out ways that those obstacles can be overcome. I have also seen the immense talent Indigenous youth possess. Indigenous youth, from an artistic standpoint, are some of the most talented people I have ever worked with.

The challenge of a mentor is to figure out how to encourage and prepare youth to develop those skills, pursue their passions, and believe that success is achievable. A properly trained mentor can help to increase confidence, help youth make informed and positive choices, provide them with an outlet to express themselves, and work with them to set short-term and long-term goals. A vision for their future.

Mentorship includes hands-on learning. In working with youth and being in the community, you inevitably gain knowledge that will help support youth and educate *you*. That's a continuation of the journey you are on as an agent of reconciliation: taking action that will make a difference in somebody else's life while enriching your own.

There are Indigenous mentorship programs in various industries as well as in academic settings. They are available from province to province, and through national organizations like Indspire, which helps to connect you with a mentee that has similar interests and ambitions.

Every time I stand in front of Indigenous youth (all youth, for that matter) when I visit a class, I let them know that any one of them can do what I do if writing is something they are interested in. And even if it isn't, I help them to understand the steps I took, the hard work it required, and the passion I found that inspired me to get to where I am today. I do that because these things are transferable; they reach beyond a career in writing to any discipline.

I used to say that there was nothing special about me, and that's why what I am doing is possible for anybody. But now I understand that I was wrong. There is something special about everybody. Even me. Recognizing gifts is an important part of a youth's development. Knowing that they are special and that they have something to offer makes their goals possible; it helps them to understand that the obstacles in front of them, no matter how big, are not insurmountable with proper guidance and support.

What better way to participate in this walk towards reconciliation than to literally change the life of a kid who just needed a hand to help them up and guide them?

Week #22

LEARN THE HISTORY OF
THE POTLATCH CEREMONY

IT SEEMS TO me as though the heart of Western culture is the accumulation of wealth. We are increasingly more concerned with amassing money or stuff and hoarding it as if it defines who we are and our intrinsic value as human beings. It's the same reason why we tend to flaunt our wealth in very public ways. It might be in the purchase of a new vehicle. I visited a country recently where, because most people lived in flats due to the massive population in a relatively small geographical area, they displayed their economic status with cars. Nowhere on the street, and I mean nowhere, could you find a beater. Only taxis were older, and even then, they looked retro-cool. I took a taxi from one venue to another, and each time, I was surrounded by luxury automobiles without a K-car in sight (not to pick on K-cars).

I've heard the saying before that "he who dies with the

most toys wins," and I think it is a reflection of that cultural mentality. And I have to admit, there are times when I have fallen into the trap; it's hard not to when you live in what is the dominant Western society. I'm not a car guy—my wife made me get a reasonable-looking car so that when I drove up to a school, it didn't look as if my vehicle might fall apart at any moment (though it still wasn't anything to write home about)—but I do like to have nice things. I collect vintage comics, and a lot of them are valuable. I don't even read them, because I read them when I was a kid; I just display them or store them in boxes. For what purpose? I'm not even sure, for the most part. I've recently started grabbing first-edition copies of books I love so I can show them off to visitors or social media followers. I think they're cool, but there's no real reason to have so many, other than just to have . . . stuff.

Now, these are relatively small vices in the grand scheme of things, and I'd be lying if I said that it didn't feel good to have them and to show them to people. It's, as the kids would say, a nice flex. Do the kids say that? Maybe they don't. I'm approaching fifty. Anyway, a vice is a vice, whether it's a car or a comic book. And it's okay to want stuff, whether it's cars or collectables or money or Precious Moments figurines or nice clothes, but we often lose sight of what's important. We've tried to raise our kids with a focus on generosity. Each birthday, when they were younger, we had them ask their friends to give them money, and they would keep half and donate half to a charity that is meaningful to them. Cole, for years, donated to a local organization that helped underprivileged children participate in organized sports (he ended up giving all of his money to the organization for the last few years of his childhood). For years, I have donated proceeds from some of my books to different organizations, mostly places that support Indigenous education or Indian Residential School

Survivors. I have to say, from my experience, that as cool as it is to own the first appearance of Boba Fett in comics, it feels much better to donate, to give, than to accumulate or receive. That's why my wife gives so much to her family and her friends. She loves making other people happy, and always tells me that she doesn't want anything for herself (I think some of that is because I'm a bad gift-giver, but it's mostly altruistic).

Let's take a look at the Potlatch ceremony as an example of how this has played out in Canadian history. The Potlatch originated on the Northwest Coast with various Indigenous groups, including Coast Salish and Kwakwa̱ka̱'wakw People, as well as the Dene People in the Western Subarctic. The ceremony, often lasting several days, was held during important social events like births and funerals, and it involved a feast in which gifts were distributed and dances were performed, among other events. The gifts that were given as a display of wealth or social status were often then destroyed by the receiver. The purpose of the ceremony was to gain prestige not by the accumulation of wealth but rather by the generosity of giving. I've read that in the Indigenous groups that practised the Potlatch, which is anglicized from the Nootka word *patshatl*, meaning *gift*, the mark of a true chief was that they died poor due to the distribution of wealth; his true standing in the community was measured not by what he had but what he had given.

Does that seem odd? Newcomers felt it was more than odd. A social system based on the *distribution* of wealth was something that didn't fit into the European worldview, and the Potlatch ceremony, as a result, became the target of missionaries and government officials. "It is not possible," it was said by John A. Macdonald, "that the Indian can acquire property, or can become industrious with any good result, while under the influence of this mania." It was literally insane to Western society that a person's standing could be measured not by what they had but by what they had given away, and thus, the Canadian government ended up banning the ceremony, along with the many other ceremonies and practices they outlawed. Section 3 of *An Act Further to Amend The Indian Act, 1880*, states:

> "Every Indian or other person who engages in or assists in celebrating the Indian festival known as the 'Potlatch' . . . is guilty of a misdemeanor, and shall be liable to imprisonment."

Totally reasonable response to something that makes somebody else uncomfortable. *I don't like your way of living, so you can't do it, and if you do, you're going to jail.* The Potlatch was illegal for over sixty years, and during that time, many Indigenous people were imprisoned, but still, the ceremony was conducted in secret until the ban was lifted in 1951. And even then, due to more than half a century of the ceremony being outlawed, it took a long time before it came back into practice. By the 1970s, it had re-established itself as part of the way of living for the Indigenous cultures who practised it. Practising the Potlatch after more than sixty years, after what was effectively almost eighty years, was an important act of reclamation, a way to display to the world that our traditions and ways of living are not broken, just like our languages and other ceremonies and practices that were banned alongside the Potlatch. We are still here, our cultures are still vital, and nothing can take these things away from us.

To learn more, pick up *Potlatch as Pedagogy: Learning Through Ceremony* by Robert Davidson and Sara Florence Davidson. In fact, that book takes about a week to read, which is perfect for what we're doing here.

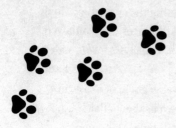

Week #23

VIEW THE SKY THROUGH AN INDIGENOUS LENS

IT MAY STRIKE you as an odd thing to do, but we need to decolonize how we look at the sky. There are few things more beautiful than the night sky and its blanket of stars. That's probably one of the reasons I like to think of myself as somebody who prefers the country to the city, whether it's out at a cottage, in a small town like Melita, where my maternal grandparents lived, or Norway House Cree Nation, where my father grew up,. You cannot see the sky in the city the same way you can when you're out in the country. There are no streetlamps that seem to send their light into, the air like fog. The pervasive darkness on the land reveals the stars and the moon in such a profound way that it's almost as if somebody turned Mother Nature's dimmer switch to full power. But the question is, What do we see when we look at the sky?

I ask that when I visit students. I'm asked out quite a bit to speak to kids about *The Barren Grounds*, and the entire *Misewa Saga* series. It gives me the opportunity to continue the work of not only decolonizing classrooms and libraries but also, yes, the sky. I often start by asking kids what the first constellation they think of is, and I'm going to ask you the same thing. Think about it for one second. There is a high probability that you thought of the Big Dipper, or more accurately, Ursa Major. Not to throw shade on kitchen ladles, but there is much more interesting lore that is associated with Ursa Major, and every other constellation visible to the naked eye. Of course, star stories are cross-cultural. They are not specific to one group of people. But Indigenous people, and Ininiwak (Cree people) specifically, as that is my background, are rich in stories of the sky. Elders who know much about the night sky will say there is a story for every star and every constellation. That every star has a name and a teaching attached to it.

And those teachings are, as well, not specific to one culture. They are not in place to only benefit Ininiwak. Some of them are fun. The Great Bear constellation, which is, from an Indigenous perspective, Ursa Major, is a story that, as I have learned, has two important lessons. One of them is about bullying. In the story, there is a bear that has been stalking an area of land, ransacking villages, and hurting the animal beings that live within those villages. Eventually, the animal beings have had enough, and they decide to stand up to the bear. As all bullies are cowards, once challenged, the bear runs away. A group of bird warriors give chase, and the robin mortally wounds the bear. The bear's blood splashes across the robin's breast, making it red. I adapted that story into the second book in *The Misewa Saga* series, *The Great Bear*, and what I have been able to do is speak to kids about anti-bullying.

I learned most of what I know about the stars and constellations from the work of Wilfred Buck, a Cree astronomer and one of the foremost Indigenous star story experts. He has an excellent book entitled *Tipiskawi Kisik: Night Sky Star Stories*, which I have read numerous times. Buck has said that he learned his first star story when he was a teenager. Just as I have learned through his storytelling, he learned from those who came before him.

Everybody has their favourite star story. Mine is Ochekatchakosuk, or the Fisher Stars. Serendipitously, Buck and I both learned a version of this story from Murdo Scribe, an Elder in northern Manitoba. The Fisher is a weasel-like animal. A significant portion of the constellation encompasses Ursa Major. The bent handle of the Big Dipper is the broken tale of the fisher. Way more interesting, right? The story goes that in an area of the world to the north, it was winter all the time. A long time ago, a man stole the summer birds, who are responsible for the turning of the seasons. With the summer birds taken, winter never left. Dying from starvation, the animal beings in a village decide something must be done. The Fisher, the greatest hunter in the village, ends up volunteering to rescue the summer birds. He travels a long distance until he finds where the summer birds are being kept, under the watchful eye of a sandhill crane. In a daring escape, he glues the crane's beak shut so that he can't warn the man of what's happening. He frees the summer birds and takes off running just as the crane forces his mouth open and calls to the man. The Fisher jumps into the sky to get away but is struck in the tail with an arrow and falls earthward. Before hitting the ground, he is caught by the Creator and placed into the sky to honour his sacrifice.

The story speaks to the connections we forge. Connections that are possible within and between Indigenous cultures, and between Indigenous and non-Indigenous people. Stories bring people together. When I was researching Indigenous constellation stories, something that struck me was all the variations of the Fisher Stars story. There were versions of it from Ontario, from an Anishinaabe storyteller named Isaac Murdoch; from Manitoba (Wilfred Buck and Murdo Scribe [who came from Norway House, like my father]); and out farther west, too. The stories were told differently, details changed here and there. In one version, it's a man who steals the summer birds; in another, it's more of an "old man winter" kind of vibe. A squirrel knows where the summer birds are being kept in one iteration, while in another, the Fisher needs to travel to where Mother Earth meets Sky World and chew his way through the barrier. But the heart of the story is constant. There's a never-ending winter, the Fisher volunteers to save the day, and the poor guy gets shot in the tail (the puncture wound in his tail is the star Alcor). How is it possible that the story lives within so many different communities, and is told by different storytellers? It indicates that different groups of Indigenous people came together and shared things with one another, including stories.

Ochekatchakosuk shares this message: if you take too much from the land, there are consequences. It constantly amazes me how forward-thinking Indigenous people have been, and are. The fact that we have stories that are very likely hundreds of years old and that spoke about environmental impacts and climate change shows that, if it wasn't known already, we have a lot to offer—both in how we used to live, and how we live now. Mistahimaskwa (The Big Bear) and Ochekatchakosuk (The Fisher Stars) are two of many stories that not only are beautifully told and constructed but also teach things that are of benefit to all, not just Indigenous people.

If you are out in the country, where the harsh lights of the city are nowhere to be seen, where the sky and its endless beauty reveal themselves to you unfettered, try sitting in the silence and calm that night can bring. Hopefully, the flies aren't too bad, but there is bug spray for that. Look up at the sky, trace constellations in your mind, and connect them to stories that you have learned. It makes them come alive, teaches us about the way things are, and, because of the connectivity inherent in stories, shows us how things can be. *Decolonizing* can be an intimidating word, but Indigenizing something doesn't exclude others from the experience that is possible with our stories.

Quite the opposite: it is an open invitation.

Week #24

RECOGNIZE INDIGENOUS INNOVATION

THERE'S AN IRONY to the history of this country that is not lost on me, and that should not be lost on anybody when it comes to the troubled relationship between Indigenous people and Canada. When you see it, it's hard to unsee. You'll be reminded of it, hopefully in a good way, on a daily basis—because this truth is literally inescapable and undeniable. I'm being vague; sorry about that. It's a delicate balance to provide context without the entire action. What I want to do with each action is to provide a jump-start, and then sit back and watch good things happen.

In this case, I want you to appreciate how innovative Indigenous people have been on this land for thousands of years before Confederation. Where's the irony in that statement? Well, consider how Indigenous people were viewed when settlers arrived in the seventeenth century. It is well known that newcomers didn't have much respect for how Indigenous people lived. They did not recognize our laws, governments, cultures, values and beliefs, social structures, medicines . . . pretty much every aspect of our lives. They didn't even think we had a right to be on the land that we already inhabited. The attitude was to make decisions for everybody, including Indigenous people, without consultation with them.

There are numerous examples of this. It's how the town of Gimli came to be. Icelanders settled in Sandy Bar around 1875 and unceremoniously displaced the Indigenous community already living there. Instead of holding resentment, Indigenous people, in particular a man named John Ramsay, did their best to help the newcomers. Ramsay showed them how to fortify their houses, how to hunt and fish, and how to make their boats leak-proof, and provided food to families who were not able to catch their own meals. He did this even though his family was wiped out by smallpox brought by the settlers, save for one daughter who was left horribly disfigured. There is evidence to suggest that some of the methods Ramsay taught the Icelanders are still used today, even back in Iceland, where he is something of a legend.

So where's the irony?

For quite a long time, we, Indigenous Peoples as a whole, were viewed as savages with primitive lifestyles. Settlers took such pity on us that they wanted to save us, to civilize us. Prime Minister John A. Macdonald famously said, "When the school is on the reserve, the child lives with its parents, who are savages, and though he may learn to read and write, his habits and training mode of thought are Indian. He is simply a savage who can read and write." This was not an isolated sentiment, but it was patently false. Indigenous

People, we ought to know now, had complex social and governance structures, sustainable ways of living, and countless innovations that were not seen because of the blindness of the Savage Indian belief. Simply because we spoke a different language, didn't wear the same style of clothing, and had better hair? And so, not only were our children taken away, but our ceremonies, our languages, and our cultures were suppressed. Outlawed. Made illegal. We couldn't even leave our communities without permission. This was the case for almost one hundred years until the Indian Act was amended in the 1950s. And even then, we couldn't vote until the 1960s and our rights weren't recognized officially until the early 1980s in the Canadian constitution.

What is the action for this week, then? It's simply to do a deep dive into Indigenous innovation. I'm going to provide some examples to get you started. Here are a few things that Indigenous people are responsible for, and many of them are used in the daily lives of all Canadians.

- **Goggles:** In 1916, an American named Charles J. Troppman registered the first patent for a "goggle." However, the Inuit invented goggles, carving them from antlers of caribou, wood, or shell to prevent snow blindness.
- **Petroleum jelly:** It's often said that Robert Chesebrough, a chemist who was also American, visited oil fields to research new materials that could be found in fuel. Oil workers had been using rod wax to heal burned or wounded skin. He's credited with the discovery of petroleum jelly, when, in fact, Indigenous people used it to moisten and protect both animal and human skin and stimulate healing long before 1859.

- **Syringes:** Around the same time, Alexander Wood came up with the modern hypodermic syringe (1853). He attached a hollow needle to a plunger. Other people have been given some credit as well, including Francis Rynd and Christopher Wren. But guess what? Before colonization, Indigenous people used a sharpened, hollowed-out bird bone and an animal bladder to inject fluids into the body or irrigate wounds.

- **Baby bottles:** By now, you will have come to expect that somebody other than an Indigenous person has likely been given credit for this invention—and you'd be right: the Iroquois took dried and greased bear gut, added a nipple made from a bird's quill, and created what we know today as the baby bottle. They used the bottles they ingeniously created to feed their infants, too.

Recognizing Indigenous contributions to society is a good place to start. That's half the battle. But I'm a sucker for specificity. I think it's always better to name things so that I have a clear idea of what I'm talking about, especially because I often share what I've learned with a lot of people. Whether you are going to share what you've learned or not (I think you should; I think sharing stuff like this is important), why don't you put together a list of ten things that Indigenous people have invented and learn a little bit about each of them? Just a note or two to go along with the innovation. I think you'll be surprised. I was. And hopefully, like me, it will beg the question: Why did we so quickly dismiss Indigenous people across Turtle Island as primitive savages?

Week #25

CELEBRATE NATIONAL INDIGENOUS PEOPLES DAY

IT'S ALWAYS NICE to have an action tied to a particular date. This is one of those times. This day, proclaimed to be June 21, to be exact, is National Indigenous Peoples Day, a day to celebrate and recognize Indigenous people, cultures, communities, and contributions in Canada, both in the past and today. National Indigenous Peoples Day, formerly National Aboriginal Day, has been in place since 1996. June 21 was a deliberately chosen day, as it is the summer solstice. Many Indigenous Peoples have celebrated the beginning of summer for many years as a symbol of new life and an opportunity to begin again, leaving burdens in the past.

Like with the National Day for Truth and Reconciliation, there is no hard-and-fast rule as to how one might recognize this day. However, there is a difference. The National Day for Truth and Reconciliation is not a day where we celebrate; it is a day to reflect on the troubled history of this country and to remember the children who did not survive, and those that did, along with their families and communities. It's a day to think of a way forward. By contrast, National Indigenous Peoples Day is a day of celebration.

Then–Governor General of Canada Roméo LeBlanc proclaimed National Indigenous Peoples Day to be celebrated on June 21, 1996. He is quoted as saying:

> Many cities in Canada are less than a hundred years old. But aboriginal people have lived in this land for more than a hundred centuries. On June 21st, this year and every year, Canada will honour the native peoples who first brought humanity to this great land. And may the first peoples of our past always be full and proud partners in our future.

Outdated terminology aside, I like this statement. It recognizes Indigenous people correctly as the First Peoples of this land, having lived here for thousands of years, well before the arrival of settlers. Again, there is evidence that Indigenous people were living in this place at least fourteen thousand years ago, and probably longer. Here in Winnipeg, we know Indigenous people gathered together six thousand years ago, where the rivers meet at what is now known as the Forks. It also describes the importance of not only looking back but looking forward together, as partners, in what I hope will be a right relationship if we continue on the trajectory we are on, committed to the goal of reconciliation.

Here are some ideas:

- Check out local listings of National Indigenous Peoples Day celebrations and plan to attend with family, friends, and colleagues.
- Spend the day learning about the Indigenous history of where you live or work.
- Learn some greetings in the Indigenous language of where you live or work.
- Seek out an Indigenous restaurant or food truck (there will be lots of food trucks if you attend a local celebration).
- Seek out music by Indigenous musicians.
- Visit an art gallery that features Indigenous art (if you're in Winnipeg, the Urban Shaman is a great place to go).
- Read and discuss the 10 Guiding Principles of Reconciliation from the Truth and Reconciliation Report with family, friends, and colleagues.

For the sake of convenience, those 10 Guiding Principles are as follows:

1. The United Nations Declaration on the Rights of Indigenous Peoples is the framework for reconciliation at all levels and across all sectors of Canadian society.
2. First Nations, Inuit, and Métis peoples, as the original peoples of this country and as self-determining peoples, have Treaty, constitutional, and human rights that must be recognized and respected.
3. Reconciliation is a process of healing relationships that requires public truth sharing, apology, and commemoration that acknowledge and redress past harms.
4. Reconciliation requires constructive action on addressing the ongoing legacies of colonialism that

have had destructive impacts on Aboriginal peoples'
education, cultures and languages, health, child
welfare, administration of justice, and economic
opportunities and prosperity.

5. Reconciliation must create a more equitable and
   inclusive society by closing the gaps in social, health,
   and economic outcomes that exist between Aboriginal
   and non-Aboriginal Canadians.

6. All Canadians, as Treaty peoples, share responsibility
   for establishing and maintaining mutually respectful
   relationships.

7. The perspectives and understandings of Aboriginal
   Elders and Traditional Knowledge Keepers of the
   ethics, concepts, and practices of reconciliation are
   vital to long-term reconciliation.

8. Supporting Aboriginal peoples' cultural revitalization and integrating Indigenous knowledge systems,
   oral histories, laws, protocols, and connections to the
   land into the reconciliation process are essential.

9. Reconciliation requires political will, joint leadership, trust building, accountability, and transparency,
   as well as a substantial investment of resources.

10. Reconciliation requires sustained public education
    and dialogue, including youth engagement, about
    the history and legacy of residential schools, Treaties,
    and Aboriginal rights, as well as the historical and
    contemporary contributions of Aboriginal peoples
    to Canadian society.

Most of all, while you do the work, enjoy yourself on this
day—have fun, make connections. And sorry about the list
within a list within a list. What can I say? Reconciliation
has layers.

TAKE PART IN A SMUDGE AND LEARN ABOUT SACRED MEDICINES

ACROSS VARIOUS INDIGENOUS cultures, there are four common sacred medicines. Keep in mind that these are not necessarily traditional medicines; that's a little different. For thousands of years, Indigenous people have used over 400 species of plants for medicinal applications. Plants used for medicine include balsam fir, alders, wormwood, wild ginger, mint, white spruce, and many, many more. These medicines are used to treat ailments; my great-grandfather was an herbal healer and was often called by hospital staff to help sick patients when Western medicine wasn't doing the trick. Looking into the history of traditional medicine is another act worth considering.

The four sacred medicines are tobacco, cedar, sweetgrass, and sage.

Tobacco is generally mentioned first. It appears in almost every ceremony and is used as an offering. You may have heard the term *laying tobacco*; it's a spiritual statement. Tobacco is offered by hunters and done so, in all circumstances, with the left hand—the hand that is closest to the heart. You will see hunters lay tobacco both before and following a kill as a way of showing thanks to the Creator and the animal. When I wrote the biography *Sugar Falls*, I included a scene that Elder Betty Ross relayed to me from her childhood, when her adopted father brought her to the titular Sugar Falls and demonstrated the spiritual power of tobacco. He took her near a bubbling stream and told her to watch, and when he spread tobacco across the surface, the water quieted instantly. If you've been to an event with an Indigenous speaker, you will often see, prior to speaking, the presenter being offered tobacco (with the left hand again). Tobacco is offered in order to ask for help, guidance, protection, or to share knowledge. I asked my father once what he did with all the tobacco he had been given over the years, and he told me that he spread it on the ground and buried the ties because he was taught that you aren't supposed to keep it. When I give virtual presentations, and I'm offered tobacco, I ask the person offering tobacco to offer it to me by laying it outside. Tobacco is considered the primary activator of all the plant spirits, the key to the ignition. There is nothing preventing you from offering tobacco yourself, by the way, to give thanks for something in your life, or to ask somebody for guidance.

Next, there is cedar, which is a protective medicine, as with another that I'll get to in a moment. In this case, cedar protects us from unseen elements, as well as the feelings that others may have. You could think of it as a shield that is there for us if we need to guard against unknown or unseen influences that could disrupt our lives. Cedar is called in for protection through ceremony, usually during fasting or a Sweat Lodge ceremony. In the latter, cedar branches are laid on the floor of the lodge; in the former, a circle of cedar surrounds the person who is fasting. There are other applications for cedar that are more directly medicinal and restorative. You might find yourself at one point taking a cedar bath, which is meant to boost circulation and metabolism (something a guy approaching fifty like me could definitely use), as well as reduce stress. If used for tea, it's a source of vitamin C. The crackling sound that cedar makes when placed in a fire calls the attention of spirits to the offering that is being made, which is why it's used, in this case, with tobacco.

Thirdly, there is sweetgrass. When I wrote the picture book *When We Were Alone*, I included a page about children who had had their hair cut short braiding grass into their hair so that they would have long hair again. This was not for poetic reasons, even though the image, fully realized by Julie Flett, is beautiful. Sweetgrass is the hair of Mother Earth. The children in the book who were experiencing the awful realities of the Indian Residential School System were literally connecting themselves with nature, with the life-giving properties of the land. This was important because the schools were in place to sever our connection to culture, which includes our connection to the land and the water. For older readers—who may have personal memories of the physical, mental, and other abuses that occurred in residential schools—the image may bring back a positive memory as well: the aroma of sweetgrass, its sweet scent, which reminds us of that connection and the love and care that Mother Earth has for people. All people. Unsurprisingly, people have used sweetgrass for aromatherapy, a scent of candles and bath salts, but for Indigenous people, it is sacred and a part of our stories, including that of Skywoman, which you should definitely read. In the story, the first plant ever grown on earth is wiingasshk, an Anishinaabe word that means sweetgrass. The plant is often used for purification in the ceremony many people know called smudging, a ceremonial practice that also includes sage.

If cedar protects us from outside influences, sage protects us from ourselves because it offers relief from internal struggles. I've used it to deal with anxiety, something that has been present in my life for years. It's funny; I get anxious over almost everything except public speaking, but I do the most smudging prior to an event where I'm speaking because it is often offered to the room. The other day, I was giving a keynote to teachers for a professional development day in St. James, and as soon as I entered the building, there was a group of four Indigenous educators with a smudge bowl filled with a bundle of sage. I'd been feeling anxious that morning anyway, and so happily accepted the smudge before walking into the school and presenting to a gymnasium full of teachers. Sage and smudging are pretty much synonymous, even though all four of the sacred medicines can be, and often are, used for a smudge. Sage is more medicinally stronger than sweetgrass, and even though they're used together, sage is used more often in ceremonies, or in preparing people for ceremonies.

What does it mean that it protects you from yourself? Many of us deal with internal struggles, internal monologue, anxieties, self-doubt—whatever stuff we're carrying with us—and the sacred medicine offers a release from anything troubling the mind, providing clarity of thought, calm, and an ability to make better decisions in a good way. That's why sage is burned, and the smoke is showered over our bodies like water before a meeting or discussion starts. Because it's popularly known as a cleansing medicine, sage is used for things like cleansing homes or sacred items, to clean the entry of a physical space or an object. Smudging, and by association sage, along with the other sacred medicines, is so important as a ceremony that hospitals are modifying policies, for example, to allow patients to smudge while indoors in designated areas. Indigenous healing practices are cited in the Truth and Reconciliation Commission's Calls to Action under the heading of "Health," which states that the health-care system needs to "recognize the value of Aboriginal healing practices and use them in the treatment of Aboriginal patients in collaboration with Aboriginal healers and Elders."

As with many things, like the concept of blood memory, I believe that the healing and cleansing smudging provides can be cross-cultural. It doesn't only work for Indigenous people. When people smudge, they are offered a bowl where burning sage is letting off smoke that billows upward as though it's dancing. They cup their hands and pull the smoke towards their body, their heart, their ears, their mouth, and their mind. This week, try practising a smudge. You can do it yourself if you have been taught how to do it properly, or you can have somebody who is able to lead a smudge help you. Wherever you are, if you stop by or contact a local Indigenous organization, they can help you with this. It can't be said too many times that Indigenous people are willing to help however they can. They will give you the jacket off their backs, even if it's the last one they have. They'll also offer you an opportunity to cleanse yourself and clarify your thoughts by participating in this important cer- emonial practice.

DONATE TO SUPPORT SURVIVORS AND FAMILIES

MY GRANDMOTHER DIED when I was very young. She died without sharing much about her experience while attending Norway House Indian Residential School. When I was working on my memoir, *Black Water*, I heard of two instances where Nana recounted something connected to her experience or that of our family. One day, she was braiding the hair of one of my cousins and told her how sad it had made her when they cut her hair. While this is not a surprise—every Indigenous child that I am aware of had their hair cut (if it was long) almost immediately upon entering one of those cold institutions— it is heartbreaking to know that Nana was one of 150,000 Indigenous children who shared that common experience.

On another occasion, Nana told my mother that she'd had a sister who died while attending a day school in Norway

House Cree Nation called Tower Island Day School. It has been an ongoing search to figure out what happened to Nana's sister, my great-aunt. Initially, very few family members, even my father, knew the young girl's name (she likely died before she was fifteen). I found out that it was Maggie Captain, but since then, the details of where she died, how she died, and where she is now (that is, where she is buried) have come into question. I will continue to work to find the answers, but the sad reality is that I may not find them.

Nana died a long time ago, and her story died with her. A likely reason she didn't share her experience while attending Norway House Indian Residential School—which, like other residential schools, was a particularly awful place to be—is that Survivors, in the 1980s, were not empowered to share their stories. They were not supported. It was not safe. There was shame associated with their experiences. Very few stories were being told forty years ago. Of course, the climate on Turtle Island has changed for Survivors, families, and communities. Yes, we are still healing from trauma, but it's not a dirty secret anymore, that system of genocide. It's out there, people know about it, and there are organizations that offer support to deal with trauma in healthy ways.

These organizations are typically not-for-profit businesses, which means they are soft-funded. Soft funding refers to funding that is finite. It is not permanent. It can be year to year, which makes it quite tenuous, or it can be, say, every three years. Better, but still, there is always a certain amount of trepidation not only about whether the organization can continue to do its work but also whether employees offering important resources and support can keep their jobs. They write grant proposals to keep their doors open, and they rely on donations. That's where you come in.

I want to tell you about Willa.

My family and I were on our way to a gathering at the legislature in Winnipeg, prompted by the unmarked graves that were being uncovered, first in Kamloops and then in other locations—former residential school sites—across Turtle Island. There was a memorial on the steps of the legislative building that included countless little shoes. Later in the day, the statue of Queen Elizabeth was pulled down. Red paint was splattered all over the statue, along with tiny handprints. It was a powerful image. It was also a very hot day. On the way to the legislature, we stopped for some lemonade at a stand that had been put up by a young white girl. Willa. She has made it a point to put up a lemonade stand every year to raise money for a cause. My wife had seen on a social media site that this year, according to what Willa wrote on a yellow poster decorated with medicine wheels, "Profits go to Residential School Survivors!" Above that message, it said, "Willa's Lemonade Stand!" and beside that, "Pay what you can!" She was sitting there in the heat with an orange shirt that read *Every Child Matters*, a cooler of lemonade on the table alongside a cash box, and a tin can for extra donations. There were lots of people there, and we, along with many others, left Willa's stand with glasses of very expensive lemonade. The next day, her mother posted that Willa had raised over $1,000 that she donated to the Indian Residential School Survivors Society (IRSSS) as well as Mama Bear Clan. By contrast, my publisher and I had pledged to donate all the proceeds from my book *When We Were Alone* to the IRSSS, and ended up donating a little over $10,000. A nine-year-old girl managed to donate one-tenth of what we did.

Action is not relegated to the monetary support you can offer to an organization. But donating to an organization that supports Survivors is definitely a great example of an action you can take. If you have the financial ability to donate, that's awesome. If you do not, think of ways in which you can fundraise to gather money that can be donated.

The only question left is "Where do I donate?"—and it's a good question. Like when you're buying an orange shirt, you want to make sure your money is going to the right place, in the right way. Unfortunately, there are people willing to take advantage of a cause like this. Doing a careful search on the internet is a good way to uncover a proper source for donations. But because I'm helpful, here are a few to get you started:

- Indian Residential School Survivors Society
- Legacy of Hope Foundation
- True North Aid
- First Nations Child and Family Caring Society
- Reconciliation Canada
- The Gord Downie & Chanie Wenjack Fund
- Mama Bear Clan

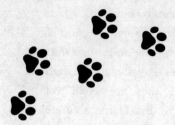

Week #28

CREATE, AND TAKE, YOUR OWN ACTION

WHEN I STARTED this project, it was intimidating, simply from a logistical standpoint. There were days, as I worked through the first draft, where I thought to myself, *How am I ever going to think of fifty-two things people can do to participate in this movement towards reconciliation?* Or if I was feeling down on myself, it would be more like, *Have I done enough in my career to present fifty-two meaningful acts?* As I got closer to the finish line, I realized that I could come up with fifty-two more, that there were hundreds of acts, large and small, and I would have to leave something out. Something helpful. But the whole point of this exercise has been to provide a kick-start, to get people thinking about reconciliation, accepting that they have a role, and doing stuff that will start to fulfill that role. So, I promise that I am not out of ideas, but I thought it would be important to leave one action blank, so to speak. To leave a space in this book for you to think of your own action, rather than be directed by me. I'm comfortable doing this because I know most people are down for reconciliation in Canada. They're into it. And there are too many people to count who are smarter and more innovative than I am. When I give a presentation about reconciliation I say, "You need to think of what you can do, within your own capabilities." It'll differ from one person to another, and how exciting is that? What can people do to walk this path, and, as a result, what can we, as a community, accomplish?

So, here it is. For this week, take a bit of time and think of your own action. Write it down in the space provided on the next page (or wherever you want to) and then **carry out your action**. That's the big thing. Because if you write it down and do nothing, it's just ink on paper. If you follow through, it's change and healing. And remember, I am always available. If you're so inclined, DM me, tweet at me, and let me know what you've done. I would love to hear it.

Week #29

LEARN ABOUT INDIGENOUS APPROACHES TO LAND STEWARDSHIP

THERE ARE THREE main takeaways when I think about the day I spent with my father on the trapline in 2018. One, my father, who was eighty-three at the time and failing, looked young again. There is no explanation for that, other than to say the water was lending him life. Two, I felt as much at home there as I did in Winnipeg. I'd never been there before, but my family had been—my father, his siblings, his parents. He'd been going there since before he was one year old, when he was just a cute little baby, cradled in the loving arms of Mother Earth. Three: This is what my father said to me. He was talking about the way they used to provide for themselves. Their subsistence. My father said, "When you were hungry, you had to catch something. Fish or prairie chicken or moose or muskrat.

If you didn't catch something, you stayed hungry." He and his family took only what they needed. Never more, never less. It was supply and demand. A technical description of this economic principle is that in a free market, the equilibrium price is the price at which the supply exactly matches the demand. If you relate that to land-based living, it means that you have a demand (hunger) and you meet that demand with supply (animals or fish). You do not exceed demand. If you do, you eventually run out of your supply.

It all goes to sustainability.

One day, my father was hungry. It was time for lunch. He was just a kid at the time, no older than my youngest boy, James, at nine. He and his moshom, my great-grandfather, went fishing. They caught a couple of fish and brought them back to camp to cook and eat. My father waited by a large, flat rock for his moshom to cook their lunch, and when it was time, the fish was placed in front of my father, right on the rock. My father looked up at his moshom curiously, and asked, "Moshom, where's my plate?"

His moshom pointed to the large, flat boulder, and said, "That's your plate."

"This isn't a plate. It's a rock," my father said.

"Creator has been shaping that rock for thousands of years," his moshom said, "just so that you can eat off it now."

The teaching was that the land provides. Just as with land acknowledgements, we need to think about that, think about the gifts that the land provides to us, and be thankful for those gifts. It's an Indigenous way of living on the land that we can all benefit from. All of this is. Don't overuse resources. Climate change is the direct result of human consumption. Human beings take too much, and greed has consequences. Since the sixteenth century, humanity has driven almost seven hundred vertebrate species to extinction. And for what? Indigenous people literally used every part of the animal or fish. Very little went to waste. My father's main job, as he got older, was to catch muskrats. His family would eat the meat, but the rest of the animal, its pelt, would be traded for money or supplies that were not available on the land. Things like sugar or lard. You are perhaps more familiar with the bison, and how Indigenous people used every part of the bison meaningfully. The bison was food. It was shelter and clothing. It was used for the hulls of boats. Its bone and sinew were used for tools, and so on. What happened to the bison post-contact? Once numbering between thirty and sixty million, they were almost wiped out by the 1800s. There are stories that tell of fields full of dead carcasses, bison slaughtered and left to rot, with very little taken. Worse yet, the animals were used as leverage; colonizers intentionally killed bison to coerce Indigenous people to comply with government policy.

Learning about our traditional approaches will help you, and as you incorporate some teachings into being a better steward, it will help others. In short, it comes down to respect for the land, what it provides for us, and what can be taken from us if we act without consideration. It comes down to reverence for the land and the water, for birds and fish and four-legged creatures, and for the connection we have to these things, because that connection is not only an Indigenous thing—it's just that we've done it for so long, and we've done it well. It comes down to reciprocity: thinking of how we can give back to the land and the water in meaningful ways, to ensure not only that it's there and able to provide for future generations, but also that we protect it and foster a healthier relationship with it, both directly and in how we model good actions for others, including our children.

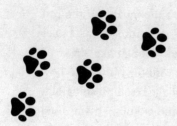

LEARN INDIGENOUS HISTORY CONCERNING AGRICULTURE

IT WAS DECIDED for Indigenous Peoples that agriculture was going to be their salvation, their pathway to civilization and being civilized (a lot of things have been decided for us over the years). So, when the reserve system was put in place, as part of treaties that were made in exchange for the use of land we had occupied for thousands of years, several promises included agricultural practices. We were ostensibly required to leave our old way of living behind—hunting, snaring, trapping—in favour of becoming farmers. Treaties promised that we would be provided with farming supplies (agricultural implements) to ease into our new lives. Like scythes.

A few things. It was never intended that we would become successful at this whole agriculture thing. That's odd. It was supposed to be a path to civilization, but supporting ourselves through farming was not allowed, so how were we ever supposed to make a life for ourselves? Never mind climb out of whatever poverty we found ourselves in, thanks to being relegated to these tracts of land that we were not allowed to leave without permission.

The thing is, had we been given the right land conditions (the good land was stolen to support non-Indigenous interests), the right seed, and the right tools, we would've been really, really good at farming. Why? Indigenous people had been practising agriculture long before colonization. There is evidence that we were engaging in these activities in the Dakotas and in Manitoba in the early 1400s.

Let's take a look at an example called the "Three Sisters." It's an agricultural technique Indigenous people have been using since hundreds of years before contact. To give credit where credit is due, the main groups I have found connected, historically, to the Three Sisters are the Seneca, Iroquois, and Cherokee. The Three Sisters are corn, bean, and squash. These crops are grown together in a process that is called interplanting, where one sister nurtures the other. The Three Sisters can be implemented on a small, individual scale, or on a larger scale that sustains entire communities (I think the concept alone—nurturing one another—is something that can sustain entire communities; this is likely one of the reasons why there are so many stories about the sisters, and why the Haudenosaunee consider them divine gifts).

Practically, the Three Sisters are grown meticulously, starting with kernels of corn that are planted in rows. Beans are introduced two to three weeks after the corn is planted or when it has grown four to six inches above the soil's surface. As the bean plant grows, it winds around the corn stalk. The two crops help each other out; the corn provides space for the beans to climb, and in turn, the bean vines stabilize the stalk. The beans also contribute nitrogen to the soil. Finally, between rows, planted squash does its job. The leaves from the squash plants shade the ground, preserving moisture while at the same time inhibiting pests and the growth of weeds.

There is more to the Three Sisters, of course. And that's where the action takes place. I am not asking you to grow your own garden using corn, beans, and squash, although you totally can if you want. I'm sure, like making bannock, it seems easy, but doing it right takes experience, and part of the fun is getting to the point where you've mastered the art. What I am suggesting, however, is that you learn all you can about the Three Sisters. Not only how they are planted and harvested, how they are used, and their nutritional benefits, but also the more cultural and spiritual aspects—like how they are considered sustainers of life. Read or watch traditional Indigenous stories that are about the Three Sisters. Learn the history of them.

Reconciliation is about more than just trauma. It is also a celebration of culture and of stories that cross and connect different communities, which seems apropos of what makes the Three Sisters so beautiful. So take the time to find the stories, sit with them once you have read them, appreciate how Indigenous people excelled at agriculture well before contact, and ask yourself some questions related to what Indigenous people had to endure within the much-needed context of this action, due to contact and subsequent treaties, that failed to recognize and appreciate the abilities and capabilities of Indigenous cultures.

Week #31

LEARN ABOUT TRADITIONAL INDIGENOUS GOVERNANCE AND POLITICAL STRUCTURES

CANADIANS WOULD DO well to learn of traditional Indigenous approaches to governance and how colonialism impacted our ways of doing things, which changed from culture to culture. By now, it should come as no surprise that Indigenous nations had complex systems of governance prior to colonization, and they were vastly different from most others on a global scale.

Take the European system of governance as an example, and let's contrast the two. The European system was designed to maintain privilege and power, to keep those with power in power. It typically holds little regard for people who need more attention and consideration. Diametrically opposed to this is the Indigenous way of thinking, which considers how people live best together and structures society with not only human relationships in mind but also our relationship with the land and the water. The natural world. In other words, how do we fit into the world rather than claim dominion over it?

Of course, Indigenous systems of governance changed from community to community, from culture to culture. Systems of governance were diverse and designed to fit. They were developed and implemented based on territory and addressed different needs—political, social, and economic. And so, the Blackfoot had a different political system than the Plains Cree. The Plains Cree had a system that consisted of a council of family representatives, while the Blackfoot had an intricate web of clan structures. The Blackfoot approach to governance would not have fit with the Plains Cree, and vice versa.

There may be a misconception that the first experience with a constitution for Indigenous people would have been the Canadian Constitution in 1867, but this isn't the case; Indigenous communities created and maintained their own constitutional orders that provided teachings, laws, jurisdictions, and more within operationalized political systems.

And then colonization happened, along with treaties.

Where treaties didn't exist, Indigenous constitutional orders remained intact. That's why you may see that in Indigenous communities that are on unceded territories outside of the numbered treaties across Turtle Island, traditional governance is in place. Haida systems of law, governance, and justice are still very much in existence. More than two dozen coastal First Nations are on unceded traditional territories in British Columbia. Interestingly, the same was supposed to have been true for Indigenous nations that signed treaty agreements. Constitutional orders were, in writing, maintained and protected.

We know, however, that the historical relationship between Indigenous and non-Indigenous people is paved with broken promises. And so, while treaties didn't cede systems of government, and the spirit of these nation-to-nation agreements was to formalize and strengthen relationships, that brokenness happened anyway. The reality is that colonial governments have imposed their will on Indigenous nations and on our political systems and have ignored the treaties and their promised protections. This attitude is what led to the next logical step for colonizers: the paternalistic Indian Act. The Indian Act was specifically designed to eliminate Indigenous ways of living, including our sovereignty, our complex government structures, and our constitutional orders, and replace it all with more "civilized" ways.

I'll give you a quick example that spans several different Indigenous cultures, as much as we do have distinct ways of doing things. Indigenous systems of governance often are participatory and utilize something called consensus decision-making. It is exactly what it sounds like. All group members are involved in the discussion of issues, and decisions are made together. This is not an approach to governance that was adopted by Indigenous societies; it is ingrained in our traditions (although Quakers can lay claim to this approach as well). What consensus decision-making ensures is that everybody understands rules, regulations, and laws, and for big decisions, such as going to war, unanimous agreement is required. If one person dissents, the plan is cancelled. Very rarely does a Chief make a unilateral decision that impacts a community.

There are a lot of *R* words that connect to the act of reconciliation, and one of them is *reclamation*. It is important to reclaim what was taken away post-contact and through the profound impact of colonialism. So much has changed, and time has passed. This means that while we reclaim things like governance structures or educational institutions, we need to consider how traditional approaches function within a contemporary framework. But we can do it. We're adaptable; we always have been.

This week, take some time to research traditional approaches to governance by Indigenous cultures, like consensus decision-making. Consider how those approaches were smothered by colonial influence, and what communities are doing today to blend the way things used to be with the way things are, and in so doing, carve out a hybrid approach that allows us to imagine a very different, and much better, future.

Week #32

VISIT A CULTURAL CENTRE

WHEN MY YOUNGEST kid wasn't even a year old yet, my family and I went on a trip out west. We drove all the way, and, with one exception, camped every night (the only time we stayed in a hotel was a night when we got in late and had to wake up early to catch a ferry). This was in 2015. James was born in November 2014.

My wife, Jill, planned the whole thing, including the activities we would take part in, where we would be camping every night, and what camping site we'd have (we like camping by the water and in as quiet a spot as possible). Her sister, Dana, lives in Canmore, so we stayed several days at the Bow Valley Campground, but for the most part, we camped one night at one location and then packed up and went back on the road.

Our final destination was Haida Gwaii. Now, by 2015, I'd been writing books about Indigenous people for several years, but I didn't know much about the Haida Nation or their ancestral home, an archipelago just off the coast of British Columbia. A place they have occupied for more than 12,500 years. I learned about them in a few ways, and they are ways that I feel anybody can undertake to learn about a culture, or a people.

It was experiential. I learned by doing, and by being present. There is an abundance of wildlife, including a unique species of deer that you can't find anywhere else in the world. We drove around quite a bit when we were on the island, including visiting the villages of Masset and Skidegate. When passing through Masset, we saw a black bear just minding its own business at the side of the road, and it helped me fall in love with the area—I love bears. We did things tourists would do, like visit Taaw Tldáaw (or Tow Hill), and stayed on the beach overlooking the ocean, in a cabin where there was no electricity or running water. That's one thing I adored about our five days on the island: our cellphones didn't work. I spent a lot of time watching the ocean, and not knowing what was going on off the island. The papers were days behind, and I didn't turn on a television set. Imagine that! We read books, and never even looked at our phones (except for one day when I drove around looking for a Wi-Fi signal to try and find out how Tiger Woods was doing). It was the first time, as well, that I saw an authentic totem pole up close. Just being there and taking everything in helped me to come to a better understanding and appreciation of the island and the people. Experience always trumps expectations based on learned perceptions, without exception.

We met people. Whenever we had the opportunity, I took time to chat with people I met on the island to get a good sense of the culture and the history. That's how I learned about the deer that are particular to Haida Gwaii. The name of the deer is the Sitka black-tailed deer. They've been introduced to

Graham Island, the largest area on Haida Gwaii, on numerous occasions, and since they have no natural predators, they've done damage to the island's vegetation. There are a lot of them, and I have to say, even though they cause trouble, they are super-cute little guys. I met people at Taaw Tldáaw; at a gas station we found when we were running low and worried we might run out; at a grocery store in Masset; at some shops farther south on the island. You learn a lot when you take the time to talk to people. Definitely seek to experience and be open to conversations and building relationships.

There are also a lot of cultural centres across Turtle Island that offer people a chance to connect. Many of them, if not all of them, provide an opportunity to learn about history as it pertains to one cultural group, or many; to become immersed in culture in a meaningful and respectful way; to learn some words in another language; to see traditional activities that have been done in the past and that are still being practised; to hear and read stories that teach you about values, beliefs, ways of living, and so much more. It is a practice of acknowledging and appreciating diversity and a way to learn about the many Indigenous communities that have been a part of this country historically but, more importantly, are still here. In some instances, cultural centres not only prepare an experience within the walls of a building but take you to historic sites and allow you, with a guide, to walk in the footsteps of those who came before you, of those who have been, and will always be, here.

At any given point, there are Indigenous communities near where you are, living on unceded or treaty land. As an example, I live in Winnipeg. Within two hours, there are a multitude of reserves and communities, from Peguis First Nation to St. Laurent to Fisher River Cree Nation to Long Plain to Roseau River to Brokenhead Ojibway Nation. Some of them have cultural centres in the community or walks that you can go on that are open to the public. If they do not have a dedicated cultural centre, there are places in the city that I can visit, which include the communities that are our neighbours. Winnipeg has the Manitoba Indigenous Cultural Education Centre, which has artifacts, books, and information about Indigenous Peoples and communities, and history on display for anybody to see and learn from. There are people in the centres who are there to guide you and answer questions that you might have for them.

When we were in Haida Gwaii, we spent a long time at the Haida Heritage Centre, which is located at K̲ay 'Llnagaay, or "Sea-Lion Town," an ancient village site. It's on the way from the ferry to Masset. It is a large building that houses a museum, performance house, carving shed, canoe house, teaching centre, classrooms, and more. It is literally rich in culture. Part of its mission statement is to foster Haida culture "by reaffirming our traditions and beliefs, encouraging artistic expression, and serving as a keeper of all that we are." I think most cultural centres have a similar goal, although it may be worded differently. To preserve culture, and to share it with others for the benefit of everybody.

After spending a few hours there, and buying a few stickers for my laptop (that's the other thing that is important: supporting the community by paying the admission and buying merchandise that not only is beautiful and made with craftsmanship but can also provide a way for you to teach others what you may have learned in spending time in such a place), we left the centre with a deeper understanding of the people and their history, and when we drove through Masset later on, we were able to contextualize that visit in a profound way.

These places are not hard to find. There are sites online that list many of the centres that are in Canada alone.

Destination Canada lists a few, including Wanuskewin Heritage Park, Tourisme Wendake, Membertou Heritage Park, Kawnlin Dün Cultural Centre, and Metepenagiag Heritage Park. They are beautiful, informative, experiential spaces. Families go on outings all the time, so this week, add a cultural centre near you to the calendar, and spend some time engaging and learning.

VISIT A LOCAL INDIGENOUS RESTAURANT

EVERY FAMILY I know has some sort of tradition that centres around food. Of course, the tradition is different from family to family. For my family, over the years, we have had certain staples in our diet that have come and gone. A long time ago, when I was younger, and my metabolism was better, and I ate meat, we used to go to a restaurant called Connie's Corner on Main Street in Winnipeg once a week with my parents-in-law. I'd order this meal called the Mad Trapper, and it was full of shredded hash browns, eggs, bannock, and three different kinds of meat—bacon, sausages, and I kind of want to say hot dogs, but I don't quite remember, and unfortunately, Connie's Corner is no longer open.

The Mad Trapper was a huge meal; I have no idea how I finished it. My appetite isn't what it used to be (that's probably a good thing). For a long time, we had what we called

Tofu Tuesdays. Quite simply, every Tuesday, we would eat a meal that incorporated tofu. We don't do that anymore, and I suppose it's because we have tofu often, so there's nothing really special about having it on Tuesdays. One thing that has remained a tradition for a while now is pizza night. Every Friday, we either order in or Jill makes pizza from scratch (more often than not, we're eating homemade pizza rather than from a delivery place). It's a fun thing for the kids to look forward to, and since I'm the one who does the dishes, I appreciate the easy cleanup. Everybody wins!

In this journey, there has been some tough work, and I know that it can be draining. It's not cultural that some things are good medicine, aside from, you know, medicine. Laughter definitely is. Food is, too. So, rather than read a book this week, or research history, or fundraise, why not go out to eat with the family?

There are different types of Indigenous cuisines. We don't all eat pemmican, which is a highly nutritious meal made from powdered meat, melted fat, and berries. The territory we occupied dictated the food we ate. Depending on where you are in Canada, you're going to be eating a different kind of Indigenous meal. For example, in Winnipeg, there's Feast, an Indigenous-owned café and bistro with deadly food (deadly in that good way). Here in the plains, you will find a healthy amount of wild rice, bison meat, fish (like pickerel), bannock (of course), salmon, berries . . . Plains Cree/Anishinaabe type of food. Bison was the main source of food for many Indigenous people on the plains, along with berries, fish, bannock, and wild rice. So, the menu at Feast, while excellent, to the informed, is kind of predictable. I'd call it comfort food.

But what if you went to the Pacific Northwest, home of many Indigenous Peoples, including the Nuu-chah-nulth,

Kwakwaka'wakw, Haida, Coast Salish, and Haisla? You wouldn't be having a lot of bison. There'd be fish and berries—there are things that seem to be relatively universal. You're going to get salmon on your plate and moose and elk and caribou. We have most of that in Manitoba. But aside from that, there'll be options that include wild mushrooms, potatoes, kale, and wild plants like fiddlehead ferns. There are probably a couple of other things that are mostly available from coast to coast, but the only other commonality is that when prepared traditionally by people who know what they're doing, your meal is going to be delicious and good for you.

No matter where you are, I am going to assume that, not too far away, there will be a place to enjoy Indigenous cuisine. There are good resources online. But a snapshot includes: Salmon n' Bannock in Vancouver, British Columbia; Tee Pee Treats in Edmonton, Alberta; the Anishinaabe Shack in Newcastle, Ontario; the aforementioned Feast Café and Bistro in Winnipeg, Manitoba; Roundhouse Café in Montreal, Quebec; Thunderbird Café in Whistler, British Columbia; Naagan, A Foraged Feast in Owen Sound, Ontario; Tea N Bannock in Toronto, Ontario; Bistro on Notre Dame in Winnipeg, Manitoba; and Manoomin Restaurant in Winnipeg, Manitoba. And that's just a few of many. In short, an Indigenous restaurant is not hard to find.

Week #34

ATTEND A POWWOW

WHAT IS A powwow, anyway? Contrary to a common and ignorant idiom, having a powwow is not participating in an informal meeting at the office. But they aren't the same as they used to be either. Prior to 1876, powwows were a ceremony to mark alliances with other tribes or to celebrate a good hunt. They typically occurred once a year, an occasion where people would drum, dance, eat food, and heal. But with the introduction that year of the Indian Act—a piece of legislation widely recognized as racist—various Indigenous ceremonies (as well as the Potlatch, Ghost Dance, and Sun Dance) were outlawed. This lasted until 1951, when some of the discriminatory sections were removed. Today, powwows are acts of reclamation that help maintain connections to traditions, songs, regalia, and community.

And you're welcome to join in!

It doesn't matter if you're non-Indigenous. If you've been hesitant to go because you're worried that you might say or do the wrong thing, don't overthink it. I cannot repeat this enough: it's okay to make mistakes—just be open to being corrected.

Nobody's going to yell at you.

Promise.

There really aren't any hard-and-fast rules, as there are in traditional ceremonies such as the Sweat Lodge. For the most part, it's just about being respectful. But here are a few basics to get you started: Don't bring alcohol. Do pack a lawn chair or a blanket. Being comfortable is allowed! If there's a circle that's been cleared by a crowd, walking through it is considered rude. There's probably dancing going on in the middle.

Keep in mind that Indigenous people aren't there to perform for you, so ask permission before you take pictures. And even if you are allowed to, don't stop dancers and ask to take a selfie with them, and don't call their regalia a "costume." Regalia is traditional clothing worn by Indigenous people for ceremonies like powwows. Stand for the Grand Entry, where an Elder will lead dancers into the arena. If an eagle feather falls on the ground, don't pick it up. It's guarded until it can be properly retrieved and returned to its owner.

When in doubt, watch the crowd. Do what they do. Oh, and bring some cash so you can try some food. If I ate meat or gluten, I'd start with a bannock burger or a bannock taco. Really, anything with bannock.

Powwows aren't hard to find. Search online for sites that publish the powwow trail. Communities have set dates so that dancers can do a tour across Turtle Island, and they try hard not to overlap with each other.

Hope to see you there!

Week #35

ATTEND A DEMONSTRATION OR GATHERING

UNLIKE THE NATIONAL Day for Truth and Reconciliation, which you can mark on your calendar and plan an action for during the week surrounding it, this is one you will have to fit in if it happens. The unfortunate problem, from a negative perspective, is that while a demonstration or a gathering is not a certainty, it is likely. Why unfortunate? Typically, in the last several years, demonstrations and gatherings have occurred in response to an event that has had a traumatic impact.

A few that my family went to stick out in my mind. In July 2014, a fifteen-year-old girl, Tina Fontaine, went missing. She had contact with authorities and services that were supposed to protect her into August, but her body was found on August 17th, wrapped in plastic and a duvet cover in Winnipeg's Red River. Raymond Cormier, fifty-three, was charged with her murder but was ultimately acquitted on February 22, 2018.

This acquittal came on the heels of the acquittal of a man named Gerald Stanley, who unquestionably shot a young man named Colten Boushie in the back of the head. Stanley's acquittal was arguably more problematic than Cormier's. An all-white jury let Stanley walk, and prosecutors declined to appeal (although the verdict did lead to abolishing peremptory challenges—the legal right that had allowed Gerald Stanley's lawyer to keep the jury white, which was, of course, beneficial to the white guy in his fifties).

The acquittals had a profound and devastating impact on the Indigenous community at large. They showed, once again, that the justice system's treatment of Indigenous people is not equitable. You can draw a very clear connection from these two cases to the deaths of J.J. Harper and Helen Betty Osborne, both murdered, and both given very little justice even though evidence was clear as to who was responsible for their deaths.

"I'm ashamed to be Canadian on a day like today," an attendee at a march to Reconciliation Bridge remarked in Calgary on February 11, 2018, in response to Stanley's shocking (but, to many of us Indigenous people, not-so-shocking) acquittal. It was one of many marches across Turtle Island held in response to the verdict, where marchers held up signs that read "Justice for Colten" or "Indigenous Lives Matter" or that asked relevant questions like "How Much Is Your Life Worth?" When Tina Fontaine's trial ended with another shocking acquittal, it was too much. In late February, on the 23rd in Winnipeg, a crowd marched for change in honour of Tina Fontaine, but for many, including for my family, Boushie was not far from mind. My wife and children attended that march; my wife made sure of that. Meanwhile, I was in Norway House Cree Nation, keeping tabs on what was happening in my home community, while doing work with youth at Jack River School, talking to Cree kids who now had to question whether their lives meant as much as the lives of non-Indigenous kids.

"What do I say to these kids?" I asked on social media, because the focus of the talks was not supposed to be the value placed on their lives, even though historically, it's a valid topic of conversation.

"Tell them that they are loved and that they matter," my friend Cherie Dimaline told me.

That's what I did. While my wife marched with our daughters to honour Tina Fontaine, I took the opportunity to tell every classroom I spoke to that day that their lives mattered. Somebody had to, because what they were seeing—and make no mistake, they saw it—told them otherwise.

Three years later, unmarked graves began to be "discovered" in Canada, starting in British Columbia, announced by Tk'emlúps te Secwépemc at the site of the former Kamloops Indian Residential School. The remains of approximately 200 bodies were found, many of which were likely children, and this number has since grown to over 1,800 across the country. There were unmarked graves on the grounds of schools in Canada. I'm going to guess that your child's school does not have a graveyard, but I do not want to assume. (Note that I wrote the word *discovered* in quotation marks, because it has been known for years by Indigenous communities that children were buried at residential school sites, and this cannot be stated enough.)

In response, once more, all over Canada, people came out and marched to honour Survivors and those who did not survive the horrors of the Indian Residential School System. Unlike during the large gathering in Winnipeg for Tina Fontaine, with Colten Boushie close to everybody's hearts, I was there with my family as we marched this time, landing up at the Legislative Building in downtown Winnipeg. The reason for the march was, in some way, different for everybody who was there, but the overall sentiment was that the children who had been discovered and those who had not yet been discovered needed to be memorialized and remembered. But more than that, there needed to be change. There was a demand for change. That's why statues were toppled. That's why some churches were burned (which I do not condone, but I also cannot judge acts like that made from a place of deep pain and anger). That's why protests, from a societal standpoint, were happening from coast to coast.

Ignore the politics of it all, if that's appropriate (I think books are inherently political). Ignore the media's biased coverage of the marches and the discoveries of graves (it's ironic, however, that right-wing media outlets called the actions of some protestors violent—which painted all the protestors violent—but did not use that description for the deaths, many of which were direct or indirect murders). Here is what I noticed while I marched with my family and while we gathered on the grounds of the Legislative Building. It is the same thing I noticed when I watched coverage of the march for Tina Fontaine after the acquittal of that man (I can only write his name so many times). It's the same thing I notice at every gathering I attend that has been connected to the Indigenous experience in Canada.

It is not just Indigenous people at these gatherings, at these protests, at these demonstrations. It is everybody. People from every walk of life. People from different cultural backgrounds, different gender identities, different ages, different clothing styles, tattoos, no tattoos, black hair, white hair, red hair. That's what gives me hope, even in very dark times. It tells me that while there are problems, serious problems, that need to be addressed in this country, the majority of Canadians are walking with us. Literally and figuratively.

It is likely that, at some point during the year, there will be another opportunity to gather. It may very well be as a result of something bad that has happened to Indigenous people or Indigenous communities. Maybe it'll be something to do with land, or maybe it'll be something to do with Missing and Murdered Indigenous Women, Girls, and Two-Spirit People (MMIWG2S), or maybe it'll be something to do with another death in an emergency room waiting area at a hospital (there was one this week in Winnipeg). There may be a gathering for something positive, too. But even if it is negative, you can help to make it a positive simply by showing up and walking with us. It's an outward expression of allyship that means a lot. Be there, listen, learn, and from there, figure out what actions can come from it, depending on what the gathering is for.

But if you don't show up, there's no starting point.

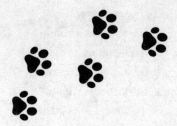

Week #36

LAUGHTER IS MEDICINE— ENJOY INDIGENOUS HUMOUR

IF YOU'RE NOT laughing, you're going to cry. That's something I've heard a lot in NDN country. I think it connects to something my father used to tell me. You see, I'm a crier. I cry often and for different reasons. It could be due to something profoundly sad that has happened in my life. It could be out of frustration that my anxiety just won't go away. It could be that I'm watching *Armageddon* (there are about seven scenes in that movie that get me every time). Or I could be just sitting around thinking of my father and, boom, it hits me.

"When you cry, it's pain leaving the body," Dad said.

Never stop yourself from crying. Never try to hold it in, especially if you think it's not masculine and you're embarrassed. In my experience, you can take that phrase—when you cry, it's pain leaving the body—and expand on its meaning. My father meant tears from sadness or trauma. Negative stuff working its way out. But I think crying is also important when you're laughing so hard that the tears come. I can't recall just how many times I've laughed so hard my stomach has hurt and tears have streamed down my face, and even when I'm having a bad day, I feel a sense of relief. In fact, it's when I'm having a bad day that I need to laugh more than any other day.

I think it's a coping mechanism. A path to healing.

Look, it's no secret that Indigenous people have faced more than their share of hardships. That's why you're reading this book. Reconciliation is required because of those hardships and the lasting impact they have had. Reconciliation really means individual and collective healing. It's staggering to think about what we have survived: various smallpox epidemics that wiped out entire communities; the Indian Residential School System, in which thousands upon thousands of children were killed and countless more suffered a hurt that has stretched across generations; the Sixties Scoop; Missing and Murdered Indigenous Women and Girls and Two-Spirit People; the overrepresentation of Indigenous children in foster care and Indigenous people who are incarcerated. And the list goes on. Yet, in spite of all of this—and it's a lot to throw at a large group of people—it is well known that Indigenous people are not only incredibly talented but also very funny (don't ask my wife if I'm funny though; she will not support this argument).

Naturally, there are a lot of funny Indigenous comedians, but even just in everyday life, if you're around Indigenous people, you're going to end up laughing, and probably a lot. I remember going to a remote community a few years back when I was still working in the field of Indigenous education. I went up with Dad, and we were attending a community feast. I was well aware that a feast in the community meant that there would be very little for me to eat because I'm vegan (although, at the time, I was still eating gluten, so at least I had bannock to fall back on). So, I went up with a few Tofurky sausages. I grabbed some mashed potatoes (I cheated, because they had butter in them), bannock, and mixed vegetables, and then I heated up my Tofurky sausages to round out a pretty good meal. When I was standing at the table looking out over the food, deciding what I was going to eat, an Elder, Victor Harper, who used to work with my father, came up to me and put his hand on my shoulder.

"Do you know what they call a vegan in the community?" he asked.

"What's that?" I asked, knowing full well the answer; it's a common joke that I've heard before, but I played along because it's funny.

"A bad hunter," Victor said and started to laugh.

Teasing is an area of humour that is common for Indigenous people, but it's not a way to put another person down or a sign that someone is not liked. In fact, it's the opposite. Teasing is a show of affection, a sign that people in the community like you. Tim Fontaine, who is the founder of the satirical *Walking Eagle News*, says that if you've been in a community for a long time and aren't being teased, you may want to think of how you're representing yourself. He lists five things to know about Indigenous humour. Teasing is one of them. Another is that it rarely punches down, meaning that humour is aimed at positions of power in order to bring them down to a level where people feel more comfortable. And it gets dark. I think that's because it's a coping mechanism, a guiding light out of the trauma that comes from facing it head-on and taking away its power or hold over you. If you watch a show like *Reservation Dogs*, you will find an incredible mixture of drama and humour. It's rare that a show can make you laugh and cry, let alone within minutes of each other, but *Reservation Dogs* does this. And keep in mind that it's completely Indigenous-created—directors, writers, actors, producers, and crew members are all Indigenous.

Take your pick. Choose a movie, watch a show, read a book or articles on *Walking Eagle News*, or sit down and watch a comedy special. Charlie Hill is one of the greats. I was watching a special that he was on recently, and he addressed the theft of land from Indigenous people. He said, "I had a heckler last time I did a show. I'm on stage, and he goes, 'I don't want to hear that crap, Injun! I'm an American. Why don't you go back to where you came from!' So I camped in his backyard."

Now, if you want to quickly break that down, it's a fact that land was taken from Indigenous people through treaties that were often signed under duress or without a full understanding of what they even meant (don't forget that the treaties were in English, a foreign language to Indigenous people back then). That theft of land has caused hundreds of years of trauma, dispossession of poverty, starvation and death, and cultural genocide. Making a joke about it doesn't diminish the significance of what it's done to our people, but it does help to heal, even slightly, through laughter. I think that we can joke about just how strong and resilient we are. And there's nothing to say that you can't laugh about it, too, even if it makes you a little bit uncomfortable. That's not a bad thing. To me, it means that while you laugh, if you dig below the surface, you can learn, too, and maybe it can motivate you in some way. This week, give it an hour or two and spend time with our comedy. Don't feel bad about laughing, and don't forget that it's medicine for everybody, not just for us.

Week #37

WATCH SURVIVOR VIDEO TESTIMONY

THE TRUTH AND Reconciliation Commission did incredible work in ensuring that Survivors were able to tell their stories in a safe place, and that, once those stories were told, they would be kept forever, never lost, so that, in turn, the history would never be lost.

I don't think it's enough to just read the final report and its Calls to Action. It's a good thing to do, no doubt, but in reading words on a page, you are missing that intimate connection of seeing somebody talk, of seeing their face, of meeting their eyes, of hearing their emotions. That's why I started out doing comics. I wanted to show people the history, not just present it in a text form. In showing a residential school and showing the abuse a girl or boy went through, you are bringing the reader on an important and at times uncomfortable journey that engages all their senses and leaves them with an indelible experience. They know the history. They will not forget the history. They will talk about the history.

You cannot change the past. I will never be able to hear from Nana—my grandmother, Sarah Robertson—about her time within the cold brick walls of Norway House Indian Residential School. I have come to accept that, even if I am not necessarily at peace with it. I'm working on my own little bit of reconciliation. I have, however, spent face-to-face time listening to Survivors' stories about their experience attending an Indian Residential School. Every story has stayed with me. Every story has left a mark on me. Betty Ross shared her experience with me in person, and it hit me so hard that I wrote her story with her permission. What I have learned, I have passed on, and that's what it's all about.

This week, I would like you to get online and seek out documented residential school experiences told by the Survivors of those experiences. They are there for you to see, and they are meant not just to document the history but to impact you in such a way that you are motivated to walk with us as we continue our healing journey because it is your healing journey, too. You can contact the Truth and Reconciliation Commission of Canada, and they are certain to help you, or you can search online for videos that you can watch—videos that have been made with the utmost care and compassion in partnership with the survivors who hold those truths. Truth, it can be a burden. It's heavy. But in learning the truth, we shoulder that burden together.

Week #38

MAKE TIME FOR QUIET REFLECTION

MY FATHER WAS a thinker. Many times when I walked into his study, I found him sitting in a chair looking out the window. He wasn't spaced out (as I kind of am, from time to time); he was trying to accomplish something. As an Elder, he told me that he was trying to reclaim knowledge he was gifted as a youth, knowledge that he lost during his experience at day school. Learning in English when he only knew Swampy Cree necessitated an abandonment of what he'd once known. He told me a story one time about when he was the executive director of an organization. A staff member came into his office and found him as I regularly did: sitting there, maybe a cup of coffee on the desk, and staring out the window.

"What are you doing, Don?" they asked.

"I'm working," he said.

"How are you working?" they asked.

"I'm thinking," he said.

This is to say that when I list this act of reconciliation as reflection, it doesn't mean there isn't work involved. It's just quiet work. Calm work. But emotional work, too.

Being in a place is powerful, whether it's home and the feeling of safety it evokes, or otherwise. You can and should research the history of residential schools in Canada. You can and should wear an orange shirt on Orange Shirt Day. There are a lot of meaningful acts that you can and should do that take us further down the path towards reconciliation. Going to a former Indian Residential School site is something I recommend to anybody, because standing at the foot of history helps you to not only learn it but feel it. If empathy is a part of reconciliation, and I believe it is, feeling is vitally important.

There were around 130 Indian Residential Schools in Canada. Very few of them are still standing, but the land they were on will always be there. Most of the locations are accessible, which means that you can go there. I encourage you to do so.

When I was researching my first graphic novel, a self-published story entitled *The Life of Helen Betty Osborne*, I visited the former site of Guy Hill Indian Residential School. The building itself had long been destroyed, but the land was still there. A plaque addressed Helen Betty Osborne and the school. Of course, I read the memorial, but I mostly stood there, looking out over the land and reflecting on the history. Doing that was as meaningful as reading any history text. I was standing where kids used to stand. Kids like my grandmother. I was able to imagine, in understanding the history, what occurred there. It engaged all of my senses. If images can show you history, attending a site like I did can bring you to that history. It made the history more real to me, and it will make the history more real to you.

Wherever you live, there is likely a former residential school site close to you. A building might still be standing, like the residential school in Winnipeg on Academy Road, just a few blocks from where I grew up. Or the structure might be long gone, leaving open land or some kind of replacement in its stead. There were nineteen residential schools in Manitoba, three of which are still there. That information, as well as the location of each school, was easy to find. I'll venture to guess that the same is true if you reside in a different province.

The action this week is simple, but that doesn't make it easy. Quiet reflection, in this case, requires work and emotional engagement. Other than that, depending on what's closest to you, you might need a bike, bus fare, or a bit of gas money. That's a small investment of time and money for what I believe is a transformative experience.

Week #39

GO EVEN FURTHER ON THE NATIONAL DAY FOR TRUTH AND RECONCILIATION

PARTICIPATING IN THE National Day for Truth and Reconciliation, known previously and still as Orange Shirt Day, can and should go beyond just wearing an orange shirt. The National Day for Truth and Reconciliation is a day that honours Survivors and the children who did not come home. If you want to walk with Indigenous people on the path towards reconciliation, this is a good day to start, to publicly show your commitment as a country commemorates a very long and very hard history. And that's what it ought to be: a start. Doing something on or around September 30 does not mean that we can check off our involvement and push it to the backburner until next year. I've always seen it as an opportunity to build momentum. To inspire people—who can, in turn, inspire others—to take action.

That's one of the reasons why I don't think it should be a national holiday. Making it one means we run the risk of it simply becoming a day off. Some provinces have made September 30 a statutory holiday, and some have not. Either way, it's my hope that if your kid is in school, the day has been dedicated to learning about history and how that history has led us to where we are today. When your kid gets home, you can have a conversation about the Indian Residential School System. If you take that simple action, somebody is going to teach somebody else something they didn't know before.

Even though we have come a long way, we still have a long way to go, and nobody knows everything. The reality is that older generations may not know much still, and likely through no fault of their own. If you're my age or older (or a little younger), there's a high probability that this history was not taught to you in school. I still remember one of the first times I travelled to a school to speak to kids about my picture book *When We Were Alone*, a story about the Indian Residential School System geared towards kindergarteners and older. It was a grade one classroom, and prior to my visit, the teacher had read the book to the kids and had had a chat about it. They broke it down together. After my talk, the teacher recounted a story to me about a parent who had approached her the day after she'd read the book to the kids.

"What did you read to my kid?" the parent asked.

The teacher was perhaps a little nervous. After all, at that time, in 2016, we still weren't teaching residential school history to very young learners. We were, for the most part, ignoring it until kids were a little older, maybe in middle school. It was new, and there was an anticipated resistance. I get it. When I pitched the idea to my publisher, HighWater

Press, which has done incredible work in putting Indigenous stories out into the world, they were hesitant, too. They didn't see how you could write a book about such a difficult history for a five-year-old child. But after reading the script, they realized that it was totally doable. Many things seem impossible or unlikely until we give them a shot. Then we see that almost anything is possible. The teacher showed the parent exactly what she'd been reading to the kids.

The parent said, "I'd never learned about residential schools before, and last night my kid taught me."

When we arm people with knowledge—kids or adults— they can do incredible things. And if we take the initiative to teach one another, the chances are we will all learn a thing or two. Having a family conversation on the National Day for Truth and Reconciliation is one thing, but the reality is that the entire week surrounding that day is filled with events that anybody is welcome to take part in.

No matter where you are in Canada, there will be an opportunity to attend an event. So, during the week of the National Day for Truth and Reconciliation, participate in at least one activity. It's a chance to be in a community, to be an ally, and to motivate yourself to do more. Because you can. Anybody can. You just have to make a personal commitment to do so—and I'm going to go out on a limb and say that it will be as enriching for you as it is healing for so many others.

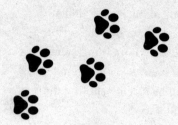

Week #40

WEAR AN ORANGE SHIRT ON ORANGE SHIRT DAY

SEPTEMBER 30 is the National Day for Truth and Reconciliation, and people certainly still think of it as, well, Orange Shirt Day. There is an argument to be had over whether a symbolic gesture is truly effective or means much in the grand scheme of things. A gesture, after all, does not necessarily equate to action, and in the end, that's what we are aiming for. We want action. Action leads to change. But I don't know; I think there's a time and a place for symbolism. I believe it has the potential to inspire change. It most certainly raises awareness.

September 30 is usually a busy day for me. Every year, I have a couple of school visits. I find it hard to articulate the feeling of walking into a gymnasium at a school and seeing hundreds of kids all wearing the same colour. It's a sea of orange, and on most of the shirts, there is a phrase. *Every Child Matters.* As an intergenerational survivor, I get emotional. I think of Nana, my kókom, and how even though she never shared her story about her experience at Norway House Indian Residential School, in some way, her story, and the stories of all the other Survivors, as well as children who did not survive, is being honoured. Because the reality is, when it comes to that "school" system, one experience is the experience of many. Every child had their hair cut. Every child was forbidden to speak their language. Every child was kept away from their family and their community. Every child had their clothes taken away. Every child mattered.

It's a simple thing, to put on an orange shirt. It's rare that something so easy can be so meaningful. But you can get creative, too. I've seen it, and it's just as nice to see. Driving around Winnipeg around that time of year, I have passed through neighbourhoods where orange shirts have been hung in the window or on a porch, waving in the breeze like a flag or a leaf on a branch in the middle of autumn. Schools have had their students tie orange ribbons around wire mesh fences that span their perimeter, and it's like countless tiny orange shirts are encircling the building. Countless, or at least more than 1,800, the number of unmarked graves that have been discovered to date (schools are intentional in their acts of expression).

What I have found is that when one person does something, many follow suit. We have influence on one another in that way, and kids have even more influence on each other. Conversely, if we think, *What's the big deal if I wear an orange shirt?* and don't put one on, others will see that and shirk the opportunity to make that small but significant gesture. And that's a shame, because it's one of those times where we come together. We all have different roles in this path of reconciliation, but on certain occasions like this one, they overlap. Everybody wears orange on September 30. It honours children but demonstrates, as well, that we are a community working towards the same goal.

One thing: Be mindful of where you get your orange shirt, because it's easy, in a pinch, to grab one from anywhere just to have one. But there can be opportunists out there, even big businesses, that want to profit off the trauma of others. So, as September 30 approaches—surprise!—a bunch of orange shirts are put out for sale. If you want to do more than throw on a bit of symbolism when you throw on your orange shirt, make sure you know two things before you buy: first, where the money you spend on that shirt is going, and second, who was involved in its creation.

Many businesses, organizations, or individuals donate the proceeds from the sale of orange shirts to worthy programs that support Indian Residential School Survivors, both direct and intergenerational. One of my favourites is the Indian Residential School Survivor Society, but there are many others to choose from. Do a bit of research and find a program that resonates with you. Then, before you plunk down your hard-earned money, take a look at the shirt itself. Many orange shirts have beautiful designs on them, alongside the words *Every Child Matters*. We want to make sure that those designs have been created, wherever possible, by an Indigenous artist. Otherwise, we can potentially, albeit inadvertently, inch a little too close to an act of appropriation. A quick Google search reveals multiple designs, designers, and even links to purchase online, or suggestions about where to go to make a purchase in person. All it takes on your end is a small amount of research. Then you can wear that orange shirt with intention and empathy.

Week #41

ON THE MATTER OF ACCOUNTABILITY

IS THIS AN ELECTION YEAR?

Canada and its governments do not have the best track record when it comes to agreements and reports. Really, that point alone can, and should, prompt another action. Look at a number of official reports, agreements, and calls to justice/ action. Read them, check the promises that were made or recommendations that were suggested, and do a bit of research to see what has been followed through on, what is in progress, and what has been ignored. If we were to pick a few chronologically, we could start with treaty agreements.

Now, it's not impossible, but with seventy historic treaties recognized by the Government of Canada, it would be tough to get through them all. Should you wish to, it might be something to undertake over the course of a year or two. That being said, just as with the Indian Residential School System, you have something called the common experience, meaning that the experience of one can be extrapolated, in a general sense, to the experience of many, if not all. Treaties are kind of the same way. In these agreements, Indigenous Peoples were to hand over a large area of land in exchange for things like annuities in cash or items such as blankets and clothing; reserves large enough to accommodate every family with acres of land; schools built in the community, if desired; the prohibition of alcohol; or the provision of farming equipment. And just as promises were made in exchange for land, promises were broken, too. These unfulfilled terms were known as "outside promises," and many took years to resolve.

Various commissions and inquiries are littered with the stuff of "outside promises." There was the Aboriginal Justice Inquiry (AJI), created by the Manitoba government in 1988 in response to the murders of J.J. Harper and Helen Betty Osborne. At its conclusion, the AJI, which was co-chaired by Murray Sinclair and Alvin Hamilton, made 296 recommendations all within the context of the justice system and its treatment of Indigenous people, including recommendations for community-based policing and cross-cultural training for police officers. Reasonable things that would help improve the lives of Indigenous people and our relationship with, in this case, police and justice officials. To date, almost none of the recommendations have been implemented.

The AJI also made specific recommendations that would help protect Indigenous women and girls, who are far more likely to experience violence or get murdered than any other segment of the population. This continues to be an epidemic in Canada. When I wrote *The Life of Helen Betty Osborne* in 2008, conservative estimates were that a few hundred Indigenous women and girls had been murdered or gone missing since 1980; Helen Betty Osborne died in 1971, a fact that suggests the epidemic had been going on for longer than most people thought at the time. And it's only gotten worse. That number has now ballooned to the thousands (experts believe the real number is at least four thousand, and the exponentially higher number is likely in part due to older cases being reported), which prompted the National Inquiry into Missing and Murdered Indigenous Women and Girls.

The mandate of the inquiry was to:

> look into and report on the systemic causes of all forms of violence against Indigenous women and girls, including sexual violence. We must examine the underlying social, economic, cultural, institutional, and historical causes that contribute to the ongoing violence and particular vulner-abilities of Indigenous women and girls in Canada. The mandate also directs us to look into and report on existing institutional policies and practices to address violence, including those that are effective in reducing violence and increasing safety.

The final report, like the AJI report that came before it, and the report of the Truth and Reconciliation Commission, was filled with Calls for Justice—some of them more involved than others, some specifically aimed at the safety of Indigenous women, girls, and Two-Spirit people, and others addressing broader colonial issues. But in reading through them, it's clear that all they're asking for is for Indigenous people, and specifically women, girls, and Two-Spirit people, to be just as safe walking down the street as anybody else. The reality is that they are not. There were 231 recommendations made, and the governmental response has been exactly what you'd think it would be if you're aware of this country's history. Advocates have called the Canadian government's progress frustrating and unacceptable; the government has said it's not a tick-the-boxes kind of thing. Meanwhile, the report literally has boxes to tick, and the actions are spelled out. But this is nothing new. Every Canadian government has been better at excuses than at concrete action.

That's why the Canadian government spent half a billion dollars on Canada 150, a celebration that recognized this country's 150th birthday, and subsequently widely ignored Indigenous people's contributions to and involvement in that history, while also ignoring the fact that we had been here for thousands upon thousands of years prior to colonization. Half a billion dollars. Meanwhile, the government pledged to end all boil-water advisories in Canada for First Nations communities by 2021. That number has been pushed back until 2025. Twenty-seven communities still have long-term advisories, which is also frustrating and unacceptable. The impetus for the creation of *This Place: 150 Years Retold*, an anthology that looks at Canada 150 from an Indigenous perspective, was a realization that we had, once again, been left out of the conversation. And we noted some big issues, including how instead of spending half a billion dollars on fireworks, the government could have spent money checking the boxes and helping to end *all* boil water advisories (they're spending only about 70 percent of what they need to in order to accomplish their *outside* promise). I don't think Canadians would've minded.

So, what's the action here? Maybe it's not an election year; maybe it is. If it is, ensure that issues pertaining to Indigenous people and communities are relevant election issues, and not just used for political posturing and then quickly forgotten. Whenever possible, check in with government officials to see what sort of progress there has been based on promises made and recommendations put forward by important commissions and inquiries. Otherwise, what does a promise mean, and what do recommendations accomplish? You cannot be satisfied with calls to action; you need to be for action itself. I suppose you can look at this as an action to *initiate* action. While the government cannot be relied upon to lead us towards reconciliation, they ought to be held accountable for the role they have and the actions they have committed to. If it's not an election year, take a moment this week to send a message to your local political representative—municipal, provincial, and/or federal—and ask them what's being done. If you've read up, if you've learned, you'll know exactly what to ask, and how to ask it.

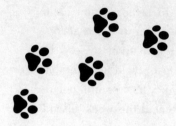

Week #42

READ THE TRUTH AND RECONCILIATION COMMISSION OF CANADA'S FINAL REPORT

THE TRUTH AND Reconciliation Commission (TRC) started in 2008 and concluded with the release of its Final Report and Calls to Action in 2015. The TRC's mandate was as massive as it was important, with a main objective of providing those directly or indirectly impacted by the Indian Residential School System and its legacy with a safe space to share their stories—both as an act of healing and as an assurance that their stories will never be lost. The official mandate for the TRC is set out in the Indian Residential Schools Settlement Agreement:

> There is an emerging and compelling desire to put the events of the past behind us so that we can work towards a stronger and healthier future. The truth telling and

reconciliation process as part of an overall holistic and comprehensive response to the Indian Residential School legacy is a sincere indication and acknowledgement of the injustices and harms experienced by Aboriginal people and the need for continued healing. This is a profound commitment to establishing new relationships embedded in mutual recognition and respect that will forge a brighter future. The truth of our common experiences will help set our spirits free and pave the way to reconciliation.

The TRC anchors the pathway to healing with the need for storytelling. It spent six years travelling all over Canada and heard from over 6,500 witnesses. It also received more than five million records from the Government of Canada. Through all of its activities, the TRC created a lasting, much-needed record of the Indian Residential School System. I feel as if it empowered Survivors and the families of Survivors and children who did not survive to share their stories, and, as planned, through those stories enabled the long journey of healing to begin.

I inevitably think of Nana when I consider the TRC and its work. I think of how important it would have been to her, and her family, of which I am a part, to be able to share her story. It would have helped her to heal from whatever she may have needed healing from, and it would have given us a clear picture of what she went through and how it may have affected us. Of course, you cannot change the past. We do not know, and our reconciliation includes the acceptance of that reality. But with the TRC Final Report and its Calls to Action publicly available to everybody, the truth is right there for you. And I am of the opinion that every Canadian needs to read it or, at the very least, its summary. While there are things we will never know—individual experiences of children who never got the chance to share their truth—it honours those same children to learn as much as we can and, as always, to do something with that knowledge.

One of the things we can do as Canadians is hold the government accountable to the Calls to Action, to ensure that as many of them are implemented as possible. Some of them are in full swing, while others have yet to be started. Yes, these things take time, but if we don't make it a priority, then the government won't either. I think reconciliation is, in the end, a grassroots movement. The government cannot lead us there, but we can make sure they do their part in terms of implementing policy, funding programming, and so on. Likewise, we have the power to elect officials who keep promises they have made to earn the responsibility of leadership. There is a scorecard on the government's website that lists all the Calls to Action and the progress that has been made to date.

For example, one Call to Action that drives a great deal of my work is under the heading "Education for Reconciliation."

62. We call upon the federal, provincial, and territorial governments, in consultation and collaboration with Survivors, Aboriginal peoples, and educators, to:
> i. Make age-appropriate curriculum on residential schools, Treaties, and Aboriginal peoples' historical and contemporary contributions to Canada a mandatory education requirement for Kindergarten to Grade Twelve students.

Considering the report came out in 2015, there has been significant progress made here. In the hundreds of school visits I have done in the last several years, I have yet to meet a child from kindergarten to grade twelve who has not been taught about the Indian Residential School System. This is in large part thanks to teachers, librarians, and parents who are accepting of the importance of teaching kids this history. Administrators are doing okay, too. While in one province, not too long ago, books by Indigenous writers about Indian Residential Schools were banned for odd reasons (for example, they require pre- and post-conversations), this is part of the growing process, and I'm seeing it less and less.

What we cannot afford is to lose momentum and interest. We can't allow what occurred with the Aboriginal Justice Inquiry, which made a considerable number of recommendations, almost none of which were implemented. This country would've looked a lot different if the opposite were true. But we need to look forward, not backward, and to look forward, we need to know. The TRC's Final Report, including its Calls to Action, is a vital contribution to completing the work of reconciliation in the long-term, so the change we make will be both profound and sustainable.

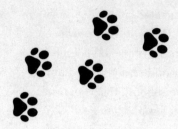

Week #43

TALK TO YOUR KIDS ABOUT A HARD HISTORY

WITH THE NATIONAL Day for Truth and Reconciliation growing, Orange Shirt Day sticking around, and during times that have provided sobering, important revelations about the horrors of the Indian Residential School System, we must prepare for important questions and conversations from young people. If you're a teacher, those questions might come from students. If you're a parent, they might come from your child. And kids ask good, tough questions. During one school visit, I was asked by a kindergarten student, "Did the kids get to bring their stuffies to those schools?" It's a simple question on the surface, but it can and should lead to vital teachings if we can handle it in a good way. But how can we do that without messing up? Without saying the wrong thing, or worse, scaring a kid? I worried about the same thing multiple times early in my career, but with experience, it's caused less anxiety. With preparation, I believe that we can have meaningful discussions that will move us towards reconciliation, not further away, because children, in the end, will lead us there.

How do we find the right road, and keep walking on it?

The starting point is to check in on our personal knowledge of the history and impact of Indian Residential Schools. The more knowledgeable we are, the more ready we can be to effectively and empathetically educate youth. Not everyone will know the history, which is a roadblock to having these conversations, and a commitment to learning will help build a foundation for change. Without a grasp of the impacts of history, it makes it difficult or near impossible to teach a child about it.

If a young person asks, "Why do we have to wear orange shirts at school?" it is my belief that adults should not only be able to explain the reason why (that Phyllis Webstad, who started the tradition, had her clothing taken away when she was sent to a residential school, including the new orange shirt her grandmother had bought for her) but also be able to connect that story to identity, assimilation, and colonialism.

I understand that it isn't a small task; we all have a lot to learn, and that's okay. If you're my age, you were never taught about Indian Residential Schools. So how were you supposed to know? There were no instructors teaching it, and there were very few books about it from the proper perspective. But in the 2020s, that can't be an excuse anymore. There are more resources available than ever before. That makes it easier to stay informed, and once we inform ourselves, we can inform others. That's the continuum. Teach yourself so that you can teach others.

Let's proceed based on the assumption that you have learned enough that you can talk articulately about the history of the Indian Residential School System. I know it's not always easy to learn something new, so here are a few things that have helped me along the way.

When you talk to a child, whether it's your kid or a student, make sure that you use language they can understand. It helps them, in turn, understand the history, and it also avoids traumatizing them. This isn't to say that you should talk down to them; rather, speak at their level. Don't tell a kindergartner, for example, that children were abused while attending those "schools," even though they most certainly were. Instead, say something like, "At many of the schools, the staff could be mean to the kids." A five-year-old doesn't need to be introduced to the reality of mental, physical, sexual, and emotional abuse, but they get what being mean is, and it's not too much for them to hear it.

That leads to another important point.

Teaching kids requires thinking about levels of readiness. Consider what is age appropriate based on where youth are on their learning journey. If a student has been educated about Indian Residential Schools since elementary school, by the time they're in high school, it's the right time to have those harder conversations. Most are mature enough, and in many cases, a solid foundation has been built.

Be precise, and use proper terminology. Note that I've most often referred to these institutions as "Indian Residential Schools," usually not just "residential schools." Keeping in mind age appropriateness, acknowledge that what happened to Indigenous people was genocide. It wasn't a "horrible mistake." It wasn't just "cultural genocide." It was genocide. Don't shy away from that truth, because it's indisputable.

While we're at it, I believe we need to stop saying that Indian Residential Schools were a "black mark" in Canadian history. They are a huge part of Canadian history that affects everybody. I see no value in "othering" Indian Residential

Schools. And really, Indian Residential Schools are not a thing of the past when so many Indigenous people, families, and communities are still dealing with the trauma they caused.

They aren't yesterday; they are today.

What about what happened in 2021? Something I've noticed is that the unmarked graves of Indigenous children have continually been referred to as "discoveries." But they aren't discoveries at all. Indigenous people have been talking about these unmarked graves, about burial sites at Indian Residential Schools, for a long time. My mother told me that years ago, when passing through Brandon, Manitoba, my father used to talk about Indigenous children buried under what is now a campground. Turns out, that was the case. The Truth and Reconciliation Commission of Canada devoted a section of their report to missing children and unmarked graves. The reality is that many people weren't listening to us, and ignoring something doesn't mean it's not there. It just means someone isn't looking.

Remember: heavy lifting doesn't need to be a solo exercise. Yes, there's work to do to learn so that others can learn from you, but there is a wealth of literature on Indian Residential Schools by Indigenous writers. Give kids books. Or better yet, read those books with them, and create opportunities to have pre- and post-conversations to decompress and break down the content. I think we need to take to heart that there is no reconciliation without truth, and that truth comes from Story.

Week #44

ADVOCATE FOR OUR FREEDOM TO READ

THERE ARE ENOUGH things to do on this path to reconciliation—far more than fifty-two—without repeating something that has already been addressed. But on rare occasions, something is too important to address in a couple of sentences and leave it at that, even if a second action associated with that topic remains essentially the same. This is one of those occasions.

In 2022, in the United States of America, book challenges and bans reached a twenty-one-year high, according to the American Library Association. The number of calls to censor particular books had skyrocketed from 619 in 2021 to 1,050 in 2022. More than 750 school districts and public libraries received one or more requests to ban a book, an increase of over 250 from the previous year. It's a real problem, and the vast majority of those challenges are what I would consider targeted—directed towards books about and by marginalized groups. People of colour, and the LGBTQIA2S+ community. As much as I have dealt with my share of book challenges and bans, my colleagues and friends who are from the LGBTQIA2S+ community, writing books about their community, find their books challenged and banned at alarming rates.

Let's take a quick look at terminology, because the sources of challenges, or the people who make decisions to ban literature, will almost never use the term *ban* when books are under review or have been actively pulled from the shelves of libraries or from classrooms. You will hear that students have had their access to some books *restricted*, and that they have to go through a number of steps in order to read certain titles. You'll hear that a book is *under review*—that it hasn't been banned but rather temporarily removed until the review process is complete. You'll hear the term *shadow-banning* or *soft-banning*. Or that a book is *not recommended for use*, but teachers have the option to choose it anyway; that it's their prerogative. Usually that's not the case, and banning and censorship are the suppression of content or ideas that happens when one person or group of people wants to impose their beliefs or fears onto another person or group. Like children.

My first experience with book bans happened in the province of Alberta. It started in Edmonton, where a web-page with the heading "Books to Weed Out" was being circulated to teachers and librarians within the Edmonton Public School system. The rationale was flimsy, but you will find this is often the case when it comes to book bans. The reasons why people challenge books never really hold up to scrutiny. This is often true because the arguments come from a place of ignorance or lack of knowledge—people who challenge literature don't typically read much of the book they are challenging; they just see the content or find themselves offended by an excerpt or the back copy, and decide that they don't want kids to have access. David Levithan wrote a book entitled *Answers in the Pages*. It's a story about a book that is challenged, and the catalyst for the challenge is a parent reading the last paragraph of a story where two boys hug and, based on that fountain of information, passionately opposing the book's use in a classroom. Levithan's novel smartly tells the story of the book challenge while at the same time gives the reader excerpts from the novel in question so that his readers get the context and content that the parent never bothered to obtain. The reason to "weed out" my graphic novel *7 Generations* was a visual inference of abuse at residential schools, and the contention that the book therefore required teachers to have pre- and post-conversations with students about the content and the legacy of residential schools. Needless to say, abuse did occur at residential schools, and a teacher's job is to discuss the novels they have their students read.

That list in Edmonton was primarily filled with Indigenous literature by Indigenous writers. Among other questionable reasoning, the listmakers often suggested that these books didn't accurately reflect Indigenous people, or their lives, experiences, cultures, histories, and communities. Imagine that. A primarily non-Indigenous group banning Indigenous literature by Indigenous writers, because they have determined it inaccurately depicts the Indigenous experience.

Not long after, *Betty: The Helen Betty Osborne Story* was "not recommended for use" by Alberta Education because it depicts violence against women (the book is about Missing and Murdered Indigenous Women and Girls), and due to problems and difficulties concerning the author. Evidently, I was viewed as problematic for speaking out against the banning of literature, and this provided a rationale to prevent teachers from reading other works of mine (the teacher who notified me of this larger list, which included other books by Indigenous authors, although I was never privy to the full list, was told to stop teaching *Betty* in the middle of her lessons about it). In Ontario, in the Durham District School Board, *The Great Bear* was banned for content that was harmful to Indigenous children and families, and because the policy of the school board was to "not teach culture," reasoning that has never been clarified to me. What does it mean that they don't teach culture? Aren't all books culture? The larger problem there is that once my book and two others were challenged, the books were pulled immediately—an action that ignored the board's own policy to address challenged literature (that is, books undergo review before they are pulled from libraries and classrooms). When I inquired about this, I was told the Indigenous policy was different (the Indigenous policy referred people back to the wider school board policy).

I recently attended a conference put on by the American Library Association—in Texas, the heart of book banning in the United States (in 2022, there were ninety-three attempts to restrict access to books or ban them outright, more than in any other state by far). But almost every state in America, except for one or two, is now encountering attempts to ban literature with some regularity. This movement to ban books has filtered up to Canada, and we have seen increasing calls to ban books in many provinces. Many of the calls—from parents, grandparents, school boards and more—are occurring in areas that are primarily conservative and Christian. And almost all of those books, again, are by people of colour or the LGBTQIA2S+ community. I don't think it's a stretch to assume that very few books that are challenged are by straight white writers.

All of this speaks to book challenges as targeted attacks, and this isn't something we should be okay with. The majority of Canadians are, in fact, not. On every occasion that one of my books was challenged or banned, it very quickly shot to near the top of bestseller lists. This happens with other books, as well. When Canadians see book challenges happen, they go out to buy those books.

Books and stories are some of the most important and lasting ways we can learn about each other. Within the context of reconciliation, they are beacons. They have already done incredible work to educate Canadians about colonial history, contemporary issues that Indigenous people still face, and the beauty of our cultures, communities, resiliency, and acts of reclamation and revitalization. The reason that almost every single kid I speak to has learned about the Indian Residential School System can be directly attributed to books (and great teachers). Where would we be now if we didn't allow kids to read books that taught them about all of these things? We would be in the same situation we were in twenty years ago. Stories have started to equip youth with knowledge so that when they are in leadership positions, they can make better decisions than have been made in the past. There is great hope in that, and we cannot snuff that out.

So, what actions can we take? There's nothing earth-shattering here. Based on my experience, here are a few highly effective ways that book challenges have been struck down, and book bans have been reversed.

- Speak with your wallet. To paraphrase Stephen King, we should be reading the books that they are trying to take away. If you are made aware of a book being challenged, go out and buy that book, and read it with your family, considering, of course, age appropriateness.

- Create public pressure. Community resistance. When you hear about book challenges, whether it's at your child's school or anywhere else in the country, get involved. Email the school division or the school directly. Call them. Show up to board meetings where administrators are making decisions on book challenges. Recently, in Brandon, Manitoba, there was a call to remove library books on sexuality and gender identity. Hundreds of community members packed a school gymnasium (the venue was changed because of the volume of people who wanted to attend the meeting on the call to ban books), and ultimately, because of the overwhelming response, school trustees voted six-to-one to reject the proposal.

- Hold school boards accountable. Make sure that they have an established policy to handle book challenges, and that they follow that policy. A good policy protects literature, because it recognizes that children don't need to be protected from literature. Ironically, school boards have it backward. Children and communities aren't harmed by access to books in classrooms and communities; it's the removal of those books that is doing the harm.

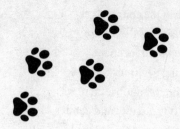

Week #45

MAKE SOME BANNOCK

I KNOW THAT I've written about the many innovations of Indigenous people and the sophistication in our ways of living, and all of that is true, but what I didn't know until recently is that bannock was *not* one of the things we have gifted to the world. The images that are conjured in your mind when you read the word *bannock*, and the way your mouth may water as mine does, even though I can't eat the kind of bannock I used to (Jill's made gluten-free bannock for me, which is very good, but of course not quite the same), come via Scotland. Bannock—unleavened, oval-shaped, and flat—was introduced to Indigenous people by fur traders sometime during the eighteenth or nineteenth century. We adopted it and substituted corn flour in place of wheat flour (I guess I could've eaten the OG Indigenous-style bannock!).

Even though we have come to think of bannock as being synonymous with Indigenous cuisine, and we as a large group of different cultures most certainly adopted it alongside voyageurs and prospectors, it should be a reminder of how Indigenous people had their ways of life changed due to colonization, including our diet. When Status Indians were forced onto reserves with very little suitable land for agriculture, starvation became a real threat. It was the main reason why Mistahimaskwa, or Big Bear, finally signed Treaty 6 in 1876, after refusing for four years because he believed the treaties meant poverty and the destruction of their way of life. In these circumstances where food was hard to come by, bannock helped—and that's not something we should soon forget.

While keeping that history in mind, it is also true that bannock has earned an important place in our various Indigenous cultures. A famous iteration of it is the "Indian taco," which, when you attend a powwow as one of your fifty-two acts of reconciliation, you will easily find. But I think it'll mean more if you make it yourself or with your family. Fair warning: it's not easy. It has minimal ingredients, but making good bannock is an art form. Just ask Jill, who has spent a couple of decades perfecting a recipe she received from my auntie Marion. Today, her bannock is known and sought after in our friendship circle (along with her chocolate cookies). It's got that soft, warm, melt-in-your-mouth quality that's difficult to achieve. I don't think there's any issue in sharing the recipe—again, it's short—because the trick is in the execution. It's traditionally cooked by mixing the ingredients in a large bowl, and then baking it in the oven or frying it in a pan. But timing is of utmost importance: when to add ingredients; how long to let it sit before shaping it; how long it should bake on either side before flipping it, et cetera.

With all that said, here's your start. There's a board in our kitchen, made by a neighbour of ours, that has these exact words:

The Robertson Family Bannock Recipe
- 6 cups of flour
- 8 tsp baking powder
- Salt to taste
- 5 tbsp butter
- 2 ¼ cups of water
- Jill's magic touch

I'll let you look up the steps yourself.

Happy baking! And be patient with yourself, because it takes work to get it just right. You have to find your own magic, and you have to build experience. Try to remember that, and if it doesn't come out just right, that's what butter and jam are for.

DON'T ASK INDIGENOUS PEOPLE TO DO THE WORK

ONCE, MY FATHER and I were talking about reconciliation, the process of it, and he said that Indigenous people were being looked upon to do most of the work, and that wasn't right.

"What do we have to reconcile?" he asked. "We never did anything wrong."

I got what he was saying. I've broken my back trying to do my part in working towards reconciliation. I've been doing this for fifteen years with very few breaks. I'm not complaining, but what if everybody worked as hard at it, no matter their cultural background? The truth is that Indigenous people *are* being looked to for answers. One of the clips I've seen lately is of Taika Waititi speaking about this phenomenon, and I love how he articulated it.

"Stop asking us what to do, how to fix things," he said. "I'm so tired of all the conversations. All of us want to be working and not having to do f**king panels and speeches. It's a great thing, it's good that we're talking about it, we have to keep talking about it, but you wonder why there is no Indigenous stuff out there? This is the sh*t you got us doing. Making us come and talk about the problem and tell you how to fix it. You broke it, you fix it."

He goes on to use an analogy of a house burning down, and the people who burned down the house asking the owner to rebuild it. The point is harsh, but it is also relevant, and accurate.

This is not to say that we shouldn't be doing any work. Not at all. What he was saying is that we can't be leading people on this path towards reconciliation when we are the ones who have been subject to historical and ongoing trauma in a colonial country. That's why, lately, when I give talks, I emphasize the importance of reciprocity. I take less time to talk and spend more time having a conversation with the audience, because we need to talk to each other. I have also stopped telling people what to do, because it's more meaningful when, armed with knowledge, people figure that out for themselves. This book is full of ideas about actions you can take, but it is up to you to put those actions into practice, and there's nothing that says you can't do less or, hopefully, more. Think of things that I haven't mentioned. There must be more than fifty-two things if we're going to achieve the goal of reconciliation.

But you have to stop asking us how to fix it, because nobody's going to heal if it's not a community effort. In my mind, and I probably can't say this too many times, our job is to share the truth of our experience. You then have to decide what you're going to do with that truth. Share it with somebody else—a spouse, perhaps, or a friend or colleague who has said something you find offensive or inaccurate, or a child or student who should be learning the truth that you have been gifted with. Truth is a gift that you do not keep; you share it with others. Or else what good is it? It becomes a secret, and we have had too much of that silence.

If there isn't such a thing as an Indigenous Problem, then there certainly isn't such a thing as an Indigenous Solution. I've sat on a fair number of juries during my writing career, for organizations or individuals, and have spent time in rooms where a group of people decide who gets money and who does not. It's not uncommon, when an Indigenous application comes up or when there is an application that includes Indigenous content, for the entire jury to look at the Indigenous person in the room, as though we are the only ones with authority to comment on the validity of the application. On the one hand, it feels a little bit like tokenism, albeit unintended. On the other hand, though, I get it. People are nervous about making decisions involving Indigenous content if they aren't Indigenous. They don't want to do it wrong. That's a conversation I have with teachers often, because I have seen a fear of teaching Indigenous content lest it's done improperly. But doing it wrong is inevitable when we're just starting to do it at all. We have to allow ourselves the grace to make mistakes; it's the only way to improve and grow. And if we're doing something from a place of knowledge, the mistakes are not going to outweigh the benefits. Everybody in the jury room read all of the applications, and everybody in the jury room had the expertise to make proper decisions, so my opinion didn't mean more or less than anybody else's. I think it's a better show of respect to make decisions and take action together than to look to somebody else to do the work because we don't think it's our place.

This is Canadian history, and these are Canadian issues. If you are Canadian, reconciliation is a shared responsibility.

Indigenous people didn't cause the problems, so we shouldn't be the ones offering solutions. At the same time, I know that you didn't cause the problems, either. The term *settler* doesn't mean that you are responsible for everything that has happened in this country, yesterday and today; it just means that you recognize that you are not an original inhabitant of this land and that you have an equal responsibility to work towards solutions so that people within your community have an equal chance at success. The more you know, the better you do. Doing is the thing, and figuring out what to do. That's a part of the journey we are on.

CHECK YOUR JUDGMENT

A LOT OF what I'm writing here is not just part of a good list of actions for others; it has also served as a reminder for me. Or, at the very least, it has reminded me that we are not all that different. I grew up in the city, and in a good area, and because of that, I can relate to some of the mistakes that are made. I have made them myself. It doesn't always have to be a mistake, either. It can be a knee-jerk reaction. A thought. A conditioned thought. We have been raised to see one another in a certain light, and that can damage relationships, or ensure that relationships can't be built in the first place.

I can say with confidence that I grew up with a non-Indigenous mindset. A lot of factors contributed to this. I went to schools where there weren't many Indigenous kids, and not many of us self-identified. I didn't. So if we felt isolated, which I did, there was nothing to pull us out of that feeling of isolation. My parents were separated, and while I saw my father once a week, I didn't learn a lot from him about my Indigenous identity when I was growing up. I understand why, but I do think that some exposure to this would have prepared me to address the difficulties that I faced. Small incidents, like when a girl asked if I was Native or not in grade eight, and I denied it. And big ones, like when I received a death threat a couple of years ago because I wrote about appropriation and Halloween costumes.

My attitudes towards Indigenous people, and towards myself—that sense of shame when I became aware of my cultural background on my father's side—was informed by the same things everybody's attitudes were informed by. A television episode. A movie like *Peter Pan* and the song "What Made the Red Man Red?" A news report describing a perpetrator as "Aboriginal in appearance." All of this influenced me so profoundly that I came to believe Indigenous people were something they were not. And whenever I saw anything that matched what I expected, it bolstered that belief. Being downtown and seeing an Indigenous person who was stumbling and intoxicated normalized my own ignorant views. I thought, *Yep, that just about fits.*

But I often think about things that did not fit. Like when I went to watch my father receive an honorary doctorate from the University of Brandon, his first of two. Or visiting my father at work and finding out that he was the boss, that people worked for him, and the people who worked for him were all highly educated. Well, none of that made much sense. Weren't Indigenous people supposed to be drunks? Weren't they supposed to be in gangs? Violent? No wonder I denied my Indigeneity! And without much thought about it, either. When I played basketball in schools with a high Indigenous population, I was always so scared. I thought the Indigenous kids would beat me up after the game. Even though we beat them every time, they never tried to hurt us or take our lunch money or whatever else I was afraid of. They shook our hands and went on their way. Eventually, as I got to know my father better and became more involved in the community, I realized that hearing things and knowing things are different. Even when you see things that seem to fit into your false perceptions, it doesn't necessarily mean that what you thought you knew is accurate, because those thoughts lack context.

Several years ago, Dad's best friend, Strini Reddy, told me a story. Strini isn't Indigenous, but he has done a great deal of work for Indigenous people. He's an amazing ally. He told me about a person he encountered while downtown in Winnipeg. An Indigenous person who was begging for money. Everybody was ignoring this person. Some were even swerving to the other side of the walkway to pass by them at what they considered a "safe distance." Not Strini. He stopped to talk to the person and, more than that, sat with them, sharing his lunch. Over the course of the lunch hour, he talked to this person, listened more than anything, and learned a lot about their life, including how they had come to be in the position they were in. In so doing, Strini was given context. He understood why that person was begging for money, why they were unhoused, and he likely tried to help in some way. It's not a spoiler to say that the person did not want to be in the position they were in. They did not choose to be in the position they were in. Life handed them a raw deal, and while some people have found ways to come out of a hole like that, others have not. Maybe they didn't receive adequate support or have access to programming. Maybe they lost their job and didn't have the training or education to find a new one. Maybe all the trauma they had encountered was too much, and all they could do to numb it out was drink or do drugs so they could get relief, even for a short while. This is not a personal failure; it is a systemic failure, and a product of a country that has marginalized and disenfranchised Indigenous people repeatedly.

What action can you take from all of this? I'm not just standing on my soapbox and ranting about something that I used to think, that I still see, and expressing how much it upsets me to see one person cast judgment on another. And again, that judgment is not always deliberate; it's ingrained in how we have been conditioned to think of one another. It's like when we see a Black person and think that they must be athletic, or we see somebody of Asian descent and think they must be good at math. The truth is that there are unathletic Black people, there are Asian people who suck at math, and there are Indigenous people who are very, very successful. I've won two Governor General Literary Awards, haven't had alcohol for a decade, don't do drugs or smoke, and live in a good area of Winnipeg. And I'm Cree!

So here's the action—and really, it's just a way to retrain your mind to consider things differently: When you see an Indigenous person, consider the judgment or perception that pops into your head—especially when you see somebody who is struggling, who might fit into the stereotype that we are all familiar with. It will take work, but wipe your mind clean of all of that, and acknowledge that you have no idea what that person is going through. If somebody appears inebriated, the reality is that they may not be. They may have an illness that is causing them to walk awkwardly or stumble. If they are inebriated, consider what they may be going through. Maybe they've just been out having a good time, or maybe they've gone through abuse in their life, or maybe their family has been impacted by the legacy of the Indian Residential School System or the Sixties Scoop. Consider it, but don't settle on it. Just know that unless you know, you don't know, and without context, we can't cast judgment.

I think that any group of people who have had to endure what Indigenous people have had to endure in this country would be struggling with the same things in the same way. It's not genetic or cultural; it's situational. And so, you have to understand the situation. If you are comfortable doing so, talk to the person. Find out what they're going through, if they are willing to share. Or share a sandwich with them and have a conversation, person to person. Or just roll down your window, say hello, and give them some change. Your kids are probably going to steal it to get candy at 7-Eleven anyway.

If we're going to do this and do it right, we need to change the way we think and the way we see each other. We need to talk, listen, and support one another.

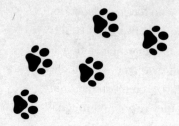

SPEAK UP/SPEAK OUT

LET ME BE CLEAR: I don't want non-Indigenous people to fight our battles for us. I want that as much as I want our stories told by other people. What I have experienced over the last couple of decades, what I've read and heard and seen, is that Indigenous people are resilient and strong and can fight for themselves. After all, it's something we do each day. We fight for our languages, our ways of living, our traditions and values and beliefs, all the things that we nearly had stripped away through the impact of various systems that had genocide as their goal. We fight for our place in various industries, like publishing, medicine, education, or music. We fight for our access to better health care, better education, better treatment in foster care and justice. Through our resistance and reclamation, we have started to revitalize our communities.

But the reality is that we cannot do it on our own. We need support. Not to have somebody fight for us but to have somebody fight *with* us, and that's a vital distinction.

Look at the publishing industry. I'll speak to it because it's the place I am most knowledgeable about, unless you're going to quiz me on *Lost* or Pearl Jam or Jim Carrey movies. The books that are being written by Indigenous writers, and illustrated more and more by Indigenous artists, are educating people in profound ways that will, over time, help change this country for the better. The space that we have been able to carve out in publishing, something that was virtually non-existent in the eighties and nineties, is because you, the Canadian public, have embraced our stories, bought them, and created a demand for more. As a result, publishers are actively looking for Indigenous stories by Indigenous creators. Speaking out can be done through creating the same sort of demand in different areas, to provide a platform for us to share our truths.

Earlier I mentioned how my books, and books by other Indigenous writers, were put on a "Books to Weed Out" list in Alberta. I was made aware of this on social media, when a person who followed me sent me a link to a post that a teacher had made, which included a website dedicated to sharing this rather large list. I raised my concerns about the list by sharing the post and commenting on how problematic it was, and this led to a great deal of media attention for a short period of time. The media's attention to the matter and the public support on social media helped ensure the "Weed Out" list was taken down quickly. In fact, in all cases where books of mine have been challenged or banned, kids and parents and teachers and librarians and writers have all come to my side to speak out with me. In every instance, that public pressure led to positive outcomes. Without other people speaking out and speaking with me, my books would have been off shelves much longer than they were.

Now, what happens when you hear a person say something racist or discriminatory about Indigenous people (or any other minority group, for that matter)? If somebody from that marginalized group is present, it's important to show support while not taking away the person's agency. It's a tricky line, but being cognizant of it and reading the room will help dictate what sort of support or response you should provide. If the person who's being attacked fights back (I don't mean physically or even necessarily with harsh words; I like to respond with kindness, as much as I do my best to educate), you want to make sure you're there to show support if necessary. But maybe the person looks stunned by the comments—maybe it's something to do with residential school denialism, and they look like they don't know what to say, or they're too upset to say anything at all. That's when other people need to step up and show their support by speaking for them. It's the same thing, really, as with book banning. When you speak out, you're essentially saying, *That's not who we are as Canadians, and we won't tolerate ignorance or hate.* Of course, if you overhear offensive comments towards Indigenous people and they are not present, which I'm certain happens more often than anybody would care to admit, that's when, if you know what you're talking about and you're an ally, you say something. My father used to say, and I have said, that if you have the opportunity to make a difference, if you have the capacity to make a difference, then you also have the responsibility.

Finally, when it comes to speaking up and speaking out, there is an element of protection to consider. Look at the epidemic of Missing and Murdered Indigenous Women, Girls, and Two-Spirit People. They are, more than any other segment of the population, subject to violence, and so even though they are powerful, resilient and capable, they are also vulnerable. I've experienced this in my own life, whether my daughters have been under actual threat, or my wife and I have been worried because we know that our Indigenous girls are more at risk simply because they are women, and they are Cree/Métis. It's the fear when felt we thought our oldest daughter hadn't show up to swim practice, because she didn't call us to say that she arrived safely (it turned out that she just forgot, but we were freaking out). It's my daughter being followed by a man when she was on a run (he left a note to her in our mailbox, labelled *To Runner Girl*, and his number was included). It's my girl being followed by a car that was moving slowly, in pace with her walking, and her having to run to the first house she saw for help. As a parent, I can't always be there. Even if our young woman and girls are strong and confident, as my daughters are, it sometimes isn't enough to ward off the evil that exists in the world. Helen Betty Osborne was an amazing, ambitious young woman who said no when four men asked her if she wanted to party with them. They kidnapped her and murdered her anyway. There was nothing more she could have done.

We are a community. We look out for each other. We protect one another. We step up when we have to because that's what you do for others who need protection and support. A few years ago, I saw an Indigenous girl being threatened by a young man near the airport in Winnipeg. I could have kept on driving. It wasn't my problem. But it was my problem. Because it's my city, my community, and she was not much older than my oldest daughter. I stopped the car, watched to make sure the girl was safe, and called the police. When the man got too close to her, I got out and told him to stay away. Thankfully, he did.

I'm not saying this to pat myself on the back; what I'm saying is that a lot of cars drove by and didn't stop, and we can't live in a community like that. If you ever see somebody who is at risk, you need to do what you can to protect that person. Of course, you need to think of your own safety, but you have to think of theirs as well and do whatever you can to make sure they are okay. That's stepping up, and that's speaking out.

If you have a voice, use it. Be an active ally who acts with intention. Build community. If we don't, our community is broken, and the path we're walking won't lead us anywhere but down the same road we've been on for a very long time.

BINGE AN INDIGENOUS PODCAST

THE GROWTH OF Indigenous storytelling has found its way into the discipline of writing, theatre, music, art, comedy, film and television, dance, and podcasting. There are more than likely other areas that I haven't listed, but I want to take a moment to discuss podcasting, because out of all the forms and genres of storytelling that Indigenous people have embraced, podcasting is arguably the newest and, as it turns out, one of the most effective.

Of course, the success of audio-based storytelling is nothing new, at its heart. After all, Indigenous people were telling stories orally from the beginning. In the same way that comics are really, as a form of sequential art, the oldest form of communication, oral storytelling is no spring chicken itself. But that's what makes it so powerful. It calls back to our traditional ways of living while at the same time embracing newer forms of storytelling. It's the best of both worlds.

It's interesting how things have progressed.

For a short while, the publishing industry was bracing for the advent of e-books. It was going to turn the industry upside down. There was such concern about the impact that publishers were reworking contracts to brace for the e-book takeover. Kindles and Kobos—reading tablets—were growing in popularity. You saw them everywhere. I remember, not that long ago, judging a writing contest and being provided with a Kindle loaded with all the short stories. In hindsight, I think it says something that I ended up reading all the entries on my computer rather than the Kindle. However, the restructuring of publishing contracts speaks to the concern that publishing companies had.

The attention to e-books turned out to be unfounded. I know this for a fact. I get royalties biannually, and my royalty statements break down how many books of mine have been sold and in what formats. Typically, the formats are physical books, e-books, and audiobooks. The percentage of my income that derives from the sale of e-books is negligible. I don't think I could pay for my son's hockey fees with it.

This is not to say that e-books are not a valid form of reading. When I blurb a book, I most often read it on my laptop, which is a form of e-book reading. And I know that many people still read in this way. It's not all that rare that I see somebody using a tablet on a plane or a train or just randomly in public, and there's nothing wrong with it whatsoever. All I mean is that what I have found borne out by first-hand experience is that physical books will always be the preferred method of reading; there's just something magical about holding a book in your hands. The smell of it. The feel of turning a page. The act of putting a bookmark between pages to hold your place for when you read the story next. What I don't think was expected was that audiobooks have been read more widely than e-books; they have become the second-most popular way to read a novel. One reason is that it's convenient. You can read a book while driving because you can play it through your phone while you're off to pick up your kid from school. Another is that it's accessible. Audiobooks provide access to the visually impaired so they can read stories just like anybody else. And with the explosion in popularity of podcasts, audiobooks have become more popular than ever.

Podcasts and audiobooks have become like relatives, members of a family. The two can even intersect. The host of one of my favourite podcasts, *Criminal*, has another podcast where she reads a mystery. So, a podcast becomes an audiobook. The action for this week could easily be that you should "read" an audiobook by an Indigenous author, and maybe you can keep that one in your back pocket, but in the spirit of oral storytelling, this week, let's binge a podcast by an Indigenous creator.

There are a lot to choose from. Just as with comics and graphic novels, Indigenous writers and journalists have recognized the reach of this form of storytelling due to its growing popularity, and more and more are using it to share their truths. It would be easy for me to tell you to listen to my podcast, *Kîwêw*, but one of the things I want to do is lift up other artists and introduce you to their work. So, you can listen to my podcast if you like—it's meaningful to me as it's a sister story to *Black Water*—but I want to offer a couple of others as suggestions of where to start, keeping in mind that you may have already listened to a couple of these, which is great.

Media Indigena is a weekly roundtable about Indigenous issues in Canada hosted by Rick Harp, a journalist with decades of experience with outlets like APTN and CBC. *Reel Indigenous* is a self-proclaimed show about real Indigenous stuff, addressing a wide variety of subjects, but giving a lot of attention to film and television, most recently releasing episodes that focus on *Echo*, *Reservation Dogs*, and *Killers of the Flower Moon*. The Secret Life of Canada, hosted by Leah-Simone Bowen and playwright Falen Johnson, is about the untold, or under-told, history of Canada from an Indigenous perspective. *Inuit Unikkaangit*, hosted by Mary Powder, replays archived Inuit stories for the descendants of the original storytellers, which is a powerful construct that reflects the spirit of inter-generational connection.

The previous options are serialized. The final two I'm going to suggest, keeping in mind that there are lots more to choose from and searching for the many Indigenous pod-casts being created today is a worthwhile pursuit, are series. The first of which is *This Place*, which is a podcast based on the bestselling graphic novel anthology entitled *This Place: 150 Years Retold*. The podcast incorporates dramatized sec-tions of the stories in the anthology as well as host Rosanna Deerchild's insightful and thoughtful interviews with the various creators involved in the anthology, from katherena vermette to Richard Van Camp to Brandon Mitchell to Jennifer Storm and several more. It's an incredible and engaging way to learn about Canada's history from an Indigenous perspective.

Now, all of this being said, and keeping in mind that any of the podcasts I've mentioned, and the many I have not listed here, are excellent choices, I'm going to suggest my favourite podcaster and journalist—someone who has really changed the face of Indigenous storytelling in many ways over the last several years. That's Connie Walker. She's hosted a few seasons of excellent stories for a couple of series (I pre-viously mentioned *Missing & Murdered: Finding Cleo*), but I am going to specifically suggest that you take the time this week to listen to the entire season of *Stolen: Surviving St. Michael's*. I have found the best stories come from a place of personal investment and lived experience, and Connie's work here addresses a story about her late father that she'd previously not heard. Connie's father, an officer with the RCMP, pulled over a drunk driver one night who turned out to be a former residential school priest. The outcome of that interaction is the catalyst for an investigation by Walker into her own family's past, and the uncovering of family secrets and trauma that have been passed down across generations. It is a powerful, heartbreaking, empowering, educational, emotionally resonant piece of storytelling that rightfully won both a Pulitzer Prize and a Peabody Award. It's one of the best and most important stories I have ever experienced, and it's one that every Canadian should listen to.

Week #50

BE A TEACHER

I CONSIDER MYSELF a writer and a teacher. Not in the traditional sense, maybe, but everything I do carries with it the intention to educate. When I am interviewed on the radio or on television, I try to educate. When I write an article as a freelance journalist, I try to educate. I don't move forward with writing a book unless I can articulate how it can be used in the classroom as an educational resource. And, of course, when I'm invited to speak at a school, I do my best to educate. I try to educate with every opportunity I get. I was just at an education conference giving a few workshops, and I noticed that they were planning to use terminology that was outdated. It was unintentional—it's a great conference with a wonderful director—but when I saw the word, I knew that it was important for me to politely let the director know there was a better term. At any moment, with every word, with every action, you have the opportunity to teach.

That's pretty much what I tell children. Everything you do and everything you say teaches somebody something. You have an influence that you probably don't recognize. And because everything you do teaches somebody something, you have to constantly think about whether you're teaching something meaningful and productive, or not. It's kind of like the discussion about wearing an orange shirt on Orange Shirt Day. If you wear an orange shirt, other people will see that, and they are more likely to wear one as well. If you do not, other people may not bother because you didn't either.

We're coming to the end of this book. Hopefully, by now, through the actions you've taken, you have become far more knowledgeable than you were previously. Knowledge is a gift, and it positions you to share that knowledge with somebody else. To educate. To be a teacher. Maybe you're a teacher already, but the education you can provide extends beyond the classroom into your everyday life. Your role as a teacher can take many forms, some of which we've talked about and some of which we have not. It can be speaking out and speaking up, not just in your role as an ally but in your ability to educate others with the words you choose to speak out with. It can be demonstrative, in modelling positive behaviour for others with the things you do and the actions you perform. It can be lending a book to somebody that you've read and that you feel they can benefit from. An Indigenous book written by an Indigenous author. It can be recommending a television show, a podcast, or a movie for the same reason. It can be writing your own land acknowledgement for a meeting at your work, one with the intention of building healthier relationships with Indigenous people and the land. It can be taking the time to correct somebody when you hear something that you know isn't right, and doing so with understanding, kindness, and respect, even if that respect and understanding isn't reciprocated. You can't change everybody's mind, but you can change somebody's mind. One person can make a big difference with a small action.

If you've listened and learned in a good way, you have a lot to offer, and you have the ability to shoulder the burden of truth with the Indigenous community. God knows there's a lot of misinformation out there that is doing damage, and so there is a lot of truth that is needed to combat the ignorance that is far too easily spread through social media platforms and popular culture. It can seem like an overwhelming task, but truth will always win. If everybody makes the decision to be a teacher, the truth spreads like wildfire. Be a teacher. Talk to your kids. Talk to your significant other. Talk to your friends. Talk to your colleagues. Talk to a stranger. Tell them something they don't know, something they ought to know. You cannot blame somebody for their ignorance if you make no effort to correct it. To educate. There will be an opportunity this week to teach somebody something. Take that opportunity, and then carry it forward and make it a habit, something that you do every chance you get. If you do, we'll be farther along than we ever thought possible. Change still won't happen overnight, but we'll get there sooner, and that change will be more lasting.

Week #51

UNDERSTAND YOUR PRIVILEGE

I HAVEN'T COUNTED—I should one year—but I'm sure that I talk to thousands of kids a year, during a hundred or so classroom and school visits. And there's nothing I'd rather do. Don't get me wrong: I enjoy speaking with adults, giving professional development sessions, or diversity and inclusion workshops. But kids, they're the ones who fill me with the most hope. Wherever we're going, no matter what we do or don't do (and this is not to say that what we do is unimportant), the kids are going to take us there. That's why I tell adults that if they have influence on children, the most important act they can take is to prepare them for the work they have set in front of them.

I cover a variety of topics when I provide classroom or assembly presentations. It depends on the school. One school may want me to talk about *The Barren Grounds* (a lot of schools want me to talk about that book), while another high school may want me to talk about *The Theory of Crows* or *Black Water*. I'll conduct writing workshops, even though it's my least favourite thing to do. You can trace that back to my anxiety and self-esteem. I think to myself, *How can I teach anybody else to write? I can hardly do it myself!* At an assembly specifically to mark Orange Shirt Day, and facing five hundred students dressed in orange, I'll talk about the Indian Residential School System. If the assembly is to honour the National Day for Truth and Reconciliation, I'll give a talk about reconciliation, how extensive it is, and the role that every kid can play in walking with Indigenous Peoples.

I get asked by teachers relatively often if they need to have a projector ready for me or if I have a presentation prepared. I rarely do a presentation with a slideshow via PowerPoint or Keynote or whatever applications you can use. I used to, all the time. Then, I'd fall into the trap of looking at the screen, reading from the screen, and not making much eye contact with my audience. I'd miss making real connections, and that's what my work is all about, so I was hampering my own progress towards a personal goal. My father went to one of my presentations early on in my career, one where I used a slideshow, and he told me after, "Why do you use those things? Just speak from your heart."

Since that time, for the most part, unless I have supportive images, I've dropped using slideshows and opted for just a mic. That way, I can wander around the stage (I also hate podiums with immovable mics, the ones attached to those bendy podium mounts). I love wandering all over the place as I talk, and in so doing, I try to make eye contact with everybody in the crowd. I like making that sort of intimate connection. The question becomes, though, how can I remember what to talk about? It's a good question, because I almost never use notes. My father was a minister when he was younger, and when I was interviewing him for *Black Water*, I asked him if he prepared a sermon for each one he gave, because on some days he'd deliver three in three different towns. Of course, he didn't memorize three sermons. He prepared one and, with each town, delivered an iteration of the same speech.

"It's impossible to prepare a speech for each presentation you give," he said, because he knew that I gave a lot of them.

I do the same thing. I have around five presentations I give, depending on where I am, who I'm talking to, and what I'm supposed to be talking about. They're ingrained in my mind, and when I have to, I pull one of them out and deliver it. If you asked me to give a presentation on writing comics, I'd be able to do it off the cuff, without preparation. My preparation is the fact that I've done it a hundred times before. But even though there is a diversity in the presentations I give, there are commonalities. There are topics that I weave through every presentation, no matter what it's about or who it's to. Writing or reconciliation, teachers or students, parents or kids. For example, I will tell almost every audience I am in front of that I want two things from them. One, I want them to live in a good, strong, and safe community. Everybody deserves that. "But if you do live in a good, strong, and safe community," I go on to say, "you have to acknowledge, as well, that there are others who do not have that privilege."

It's easy, when you live in privilege, to take what you have for granted. I'm no different. I live in an upper-class neighbourhood in Winnipeg. I grew up in a good neighbourhood in the same city. I get it. I know that I've had advantages and opportunities that many people did not and do not have. Some of that I've worked for, yes, and some of that I was lucky to have been born into. Canada touts itself as a so-called First-World country, but we conveniently leave out the truth that there are many, many people struggling to survive here. Those people live in so-called Third-World conditions. Unfortunately, and often through no fault of their own, due to the ongoing impacts of colonialism, the majority of people in Canada who live in Third-World conditions are Indigenous.

They do not have access to clean drinking water, which should be a basic human right. In certain cases, their clean drinking water has been stolen in order to provide it to others. Why? Are those other people more deserving of it? Somebody, at some point, thought, *Yeah, they are more deserving of it*, or else it wouldn't have been done. In other cases, it was the reserve system that placed Indigenous people in areas that were not good for farming, and that did not have access to things like clean drinking water, which is still deliberate.

They do not have access to adequate health care. I know of an Elder who passed away because they lived in a remote community and, when they suffered a life-threatening illness, had to be airlifted to Winnipeg in order to get proper medical attention. What could have been done during those hours in transit? Maybe nothing, but maybe something. And if there is access to health care, there is a very real possibility that they may encounter racism. In 2008, Brian Sinclair was found dead after thirty-four hours in an emergency room waiting to be treated. If he were white, he would likely be alive today, and that's a fact. He was forty-five.

They do not have access to proper education, even though in certain communities education is improving with the construction of better schools and the ability to have local control (that is, autonomy over the development and implementation of their own curriculum). Too many, though, still have poor conditions at school and the inability to attend high school at home, forcing them to make the choice to leave home or leave their education. You can imagine how parents who attended residential schools might encourage the latter choice.

There are more examples, but I believe there is a benefit to searching those out on your own. It's easy to perform cursory research to see how many Indigenous people, particularly those living on-reserve, do not have the privilege that others have, that others take for granted. That needs to change. It cannot happen overnight, but it can happen.

I tell people that if they are privileged enough to live in a good, strong, and safe community, they have to, in some way, dedicate themselves to contributing to the development of that kind of community for other people. Because everybody deserves it, at minimum. But not everybody has it. Even when you live in privilege, as an Indigenous person, you have fears that other people do not have. I have to worry more about my three Indigenous daughters' safety more than non-Indigenous parents who have daughters because Indigenous women and girls are far more at risk of violence. We can't be satisfied with that reality, and if we are not, we have to think of ways that we can make every community better, safer, and stronger with access to services and opportunities that they do not currently have. The starting point of making that happen is to acknowledge that you likely have privilege. And if you know that, and accept it, and you accept that others do not, you can think about what you can do to work towards extending that privilege to all Canadians.

You have the capacity to create meaningful change. Part of that capacity comes from privilege.

SHARE THIS BOOK

ART CAN HAVE an enormous impact on our lives and our communities. It can create community as much as it can create change. Any discipline in the arts can bring people together and mobilize and motivate them to do and be better. At a concert, in an arena full of twenty thousand fans, I've watched every individual take part in a collective motion, throwing their hands in the air in time with one moment, one note, during one song. I've been to a book launch where one hundred people in a cramped space have sat in complete silence, pin-drop silence, while a passage is read by an author. I've attended a play where a theatre audience simultaneously broke out into laughter, tears, or both, within minutes of each other. With that sort of connectivity, just imagine what is possible, what people can be engaged to accomplish.

Art can save lives. Art has saved lives. In *Bill & Ted's Excellent Adventure*, the titular characters' band, the Wyld

Stallyns, are said to one day perform a song that will save the world. Yes, it's a goofball comedy, but isn't there a bit of truth in fiction? And if art—books, music, theatre, dance, illustrations, painting, design, et cetera—can do something as big as save the world, it can certainly change a community or a country for the better.

To create change, a few things need to happen.

The artistic discipline in question—for the purposes of this discussion, let's say it's literature—needs to have something to say, something to teach, or some kind of moral to impart. If the book is able to check that box, if it has the potential to create change, how does it realize that potential? The book needs to have reach.

I am only one, but still, I am one.

What happens when one person turns into one hundred, one thousand, ten thousand, or more? We have the potential to see something special.

This book is not an action. I wrote it because I know reconciliation is hard, and many of us, myself included, sometimes think *What can I do?* or *What should I do?* Some might even wonder if it's their place to take action. We may not want to take action because there is an understandable worry that it might be the wrong thing or done in the wrong way. Rather, this book is a guide. You can flip to any one page, read through it, and maybe you'll get an idea. Maybe you will receive a prompt that will inspire action. And if that's the case, if you find there is value in the pages of this book, there is one more action that you can take.

Share it.

Tell somebody about the book. That's how it works, right? You love a book, you think a story is interesting, engaging, and so you tell somebody about it—whether in passing, in a social media post, on a book review website, or in a book club. You read it, a friend of yours reads it, they tell another friend about it, and then, suddenly, it's not just one person donating to an Indigenous organization, it's not just one person listening to an Indigenous podcast, it's not just one person watching an episode of television—it's many. And where there are many, there is substantial, lasting, profound change. It may not happen overnight, but I promise you, it will happen, and we will all be better for it, as one large community.

Thank you for reading this book.

Thank you for walking this path.

If you weren't walking it before, it is my hope that you are now.

And I want to thank you for that.

Ekosani.

ACKNOWLEDGEMENTS

IN THE SPIRIT of community, the bedrock of reconciliation, I would like to thank many people and organizations for making the work I have tried to accomplish in my writing career, including this book, possible.

I think of the students, teachers, librarians, and administrators I have met over the years. If I've learned anything in the countless school visits and library talks I've given, it's that youth want to learn. Our responsibility is to provide them with the resources that enable their education so they can do better than has been done in the past, today, and tomorrow. Teachers are on the frontlines of reconciliation and can never be given enough credit, but allow me to give you all a shout-out here to let you know how much I appreciate your hard work and dedication. And for those wonderful humans working in our libraries, keep stocking the shelves with diverse literature and fight for everybody's right to access those vital stories.

I would be nowhere without family. To that end, I want to thank my mother, who encouraged me to follow my dream of being a writer, and my father, who will always be the guiding light in my career. If youth are the key to reconciliation, nobody motivates me more to do whatever I can in my capacity and platform than my children: Emily, Cole, Anna, Lauren, and James. And ekosani, as always, to the relatives who've walked alongside me on this journey, including my cousins Shelagh Rogers and Niigaan Sinclair. But also the entire community of artists I'm privileged to be a part of. There are too many of you to name, but if you know, you know.

Thanks to Jackie Kaiser at Westwood Creative Artists, my friend and agent.

Of course, I work at Penguin Random House Canada, running Swift Water, an Indigenous imprint made possible thanks to the people I've come to know as more than colleagues. This includes Kristin Cochrane, the entire Tundra team, and all the staff I've been lucky to meet over the last several years.

In particular, I want to thank McClelland & Stewart, who worked with me to bring this book into the world. Thanks to Kim Kandravy, Production Coordinator; Matthew Flute, Designer; Terra Page, Typesetter; Adeeba Noor, M&S Intern; Kimberlee Kemp, Senior Managing Editor; Linda Pruessen, copy editor; and Rachel Taylor, proofreader. And then there is Stephanie Sinclair, Publisher. Thank you for your passion, kindness, vision, and all the hearts you put on the pages of this book, literally and figuratively.

Finally, a huge thanks to you, the reader. I can't say it enough times. We are in this together. Reading this book tells me that you acknowledge you have a role and that each step moves us further down the path to healing and building a better community. My father once told me that if we do things right, we won't see real change in our lives, but I've seen enough to choose hope, and I am walking beside you the whole way.

RESOURCES FOR FURTHER READING, LISTENING, AND LEARNING

THIS SECTION LISTS the reports and Indigenous-created works and organizations referenced throughout this book (plus a few more!). While far from a comprehensive list of resources, it will hopefully act as a springboard for your own learning journey on the path to reconciliation.

REPORTS
- Report of the Aboriginal Justice Inquiry of Manitoba (1991)
- Final Report of the Truth and Reconciliation Commission (2015)
- Reclaiming Power and Place: The Final Report of the National Inquiry into Missing and Murdered Indigenous Women and Girls (2019)

FICTION FOR ADULTS

- *A Minor Chorus* by Billy-Ray Belcourt
- *Bad Cree* by Jessica Johns
- *Five Little Indians* by Michelle Good
- *In Search of April Raintree* by Beatrice Mosionier
- *Jonny Appleseed* by Joshua Whitehead
- *Kiss of the Fur Queen* by Tomson Highway
- *Monkey Beach* by Eden Robinson
- *Moon of the Crusted Snow* by Waubgeshig Rice
- *Ravensong* by Lee Maracle
- *Split Tooth* by Tanya Tagaq
- *Starlight* by Richard Wagamese
- *The Break* by katherena vermette
- *The Lesser Blessed* by Richard Van Camp
- *The Marrow Thieves* by Cherie Dimaline
- *The Theory of Crows* by David A. Robertson

NONFICTION FOR ADULTS

- *A History of My Brief Body* by Billy-Ray Belcourt
- *A Mind Spread Out on the Ground* by Alicia Elliott
- *Black Water* by David A. Robertson
- *Broken Circle* by Theodore Niizhotay Fontaine
- *From the Ashes* by Jesse Thistle
- *Halfbreed* by Maria Campbell
- *"Indian" in the Cabinet* by Jody Wilson-Raybould
- *In My Own Moccasins* by Helen Knott
- *Lake of the Prairies* by Warren Cariou
- *Mamaskatch* by Darrel J. McLeod
- *Peace and Good Order* by Harold R. Johnson
- *Potlatch as Pedagogy* by Sara Florence Davidson and Robert Davidson
- *Seven Fallen Feathers* by Tanya Talaga

- *The Education of Augie Merasty* by Joseph Auguste Merasty, with David Carpenter
- *The Inconvenient Indian* by Thomas King
- *The Reason You Walk* by Wab Kinew
- *Tipiskawi Kisik: Night Sky Star Stories* by Wilfred Buck
- *True Reconciliation* by Jody Wilson-Raybould
- *Wînipêk* by Niigaanwewidam Sinclair

GRAPHIC NOVELS

- *A Blanket of Butterflies* by Richard Van Camp, illustrated by Scott B. Henderson and Donovan Yaciuk
- *A Girl Called Echo Omnibus* by katherena vermette, illustrated by Scott B. Henderson and Donovan Yaciuk
- *Borders* by Thomas King, illustrated by Natasha Donovan
- *Red: A Haida Manga* by Michael Nicoll Yahgulanaas
- *Sugar Falls* by David A. Robertson, illustrated by Scott B. Henderson and Donovan Yaciuk
- *Surviving the City* by Tasha Spillett, illustrated by Natasha Donovan and Donovan Yaciuk
- *The Life of Helen Betty Osborne* by David A. Robertson, illustrated by Madison Blackstone
- *The Night Wanderer* by Drew Hayden Taylor, illustrated by Michael Wyatt
- *The Outside Circle* by Patti LaBoucane-Benson, illustrated by Kelly Mellings
- *This Place: 150 Years Retold* by various authors and illustrators
- *UNeducation, Vol. 1* by Jason Eaglespeaker
- *Wendy's Revenge* by Walter Scott
- *7 Generations* by David A. Robertson, illustrated by Scott B. Henderson

BOOKS FOR CHILDREN

- *Birdsong* by Julie Flett
- *Hiawatha and the Peacemaker* by Robbie Robertson, illustrated by David Shannon
- *I Am Not a Number* by Jenny Kay Dupuis and Kathy Kacer, illustrated by Gillian Newland
- *My Heart Fills With Happiness* by Monique Gray Smith, illustrated by Julie Flett
- *On the Trapline* by David A. Robertson, illustrated by Julie Flett
- *Shi-shi-etko* by Nicola I. Campbell, illustrated by Kim LaFave
- *Stolen Words* by Melanie Florence, illustrated by Gabrielle Grimard
- *The Barren Grounds* (Book 1 of *The Misewa Saga* series) by David A. Robertson
- *The Orange Shirt Story* by Phyllis Webstad, illustrated by Brock Nicol
- *When We Were Alone* by David A. Robertson, illustrated by Julie Flett

FILMS

- *Atanarjuat: The Fast Runner*
- *Blood Quantum*
- *Smoke Signals*

TELEVISION SERIES

- *Echo*
- *Reservation Dogs*

PODCASTS

- ᐃᓄᐃᑦ ᐅᓇᖅᑲᖕᒋᑦ *(Inuit Unikkaangit)*
- *Kīwew*
- *MEDIA INDIGENA*
- *Missing & Murdered: Finding Cleo*
- *Reel Indigenous*
- *Stolen: Surviving St. Michael's*
- *The Secret Life of Canada*
- *This Place*

ORGANIZATIONS

- Aboriginal Sport Circle (ASC)
- Brandon University Northern Teacher Education Program (BUNTEP)
- First Nations Child and Family Caring Society of Canada (the Caring Society)
- Gord Downie & Chanie Wenjack Fund
- Helen Betty Osborne Memorial Foundation
- Indian Residential School Survivors Society (IRSSS)
- Indigenous Music Office (IMO)
- Indspire
- Legacy of Hope Foundation (LHF)
- Mama Bear Clan
- North American Indigenous Games (NAIG) Council
- Reconciliation Canada
- True North Aid

© Amber Green

DAVID A. ROBERTSON is a two-time winner of the Governor General's Literary Award, and has won the TD Canadian Children's Literature Award and the Writers' Union of Canada Freedom to Read Award. He has received several other accolades for his work as a writer for children and adults, including being named *Globe and Mail* Children's Storyteller of the Year in 2021, and for his work as a podcaster, public speaker, and social advocate. In 2023, he was honoured with a Doctor of Letters by the University of Manitoba for outstanding contributions in the arts and distinguished achievements. He is a member of Norway House Cree Nation and lives in Winnipeg.

www.darobertson.ca